Global Perspectives Series

# Theological Models of the Doctrine of the Trinity

## The Trinity, Diversity and Theological Hermeneutics

James Henry Owino Kombo

© 2016 by James Henry Owino Kombo

Published 2016 by Langham Global Library
*an imprint of Langham Publishing*
www.langhampublishing.org

Langham Publishing and its imprints are a ministry of Langham Partnership

Langham Partnership
PO Box 296, Carlisle, Cumbria CA3 9WZ, UK
www.langham.org

ISBNs:
978-1-78368-906-4 Print
978-1-78368-157-0 Mobi
978-1-78368-156-3 ePub
978-1-78368-158-7 PDF

James Henry Owino Kombo has asserted his right under the Copyright, Designs and Patents Act, 1988 to be identified as the Author of this work.

All rights reserved. No part of this publication may be reproduced, stored in a retrieval system or transmitted, in any form or by any means, electronic, mechanical, photocopying, recording or otherwise, without the prior written permission of the publisher or the Copyright Licensing Agency.

All Scripture quotations, unless otherwise indicated, are taken from the Holy Bible, New International Version®, NIV®. Copyright ©1973, 1978, 1984, 2011 by Biblica, Inc.™ Used by permission of Zondervan.

**British Library Cataloguing in Publication Data**
A catalogue record for this book is available from the British Library

ISBN: 978-1-78368-906-4

Cover & Book Design: projectluz.com

Langham Partnership actively supports theological dialogue and an author's right to publish but does not necessarily endorse the views and opinions set forth, and works referenced within this publication or guarantee its technical and grammatical correctness. Langham Partnership does not accept any responsibility or liability to persons or property as a consequence of the reading, use or interpretation of its published content.

James Kombo makes a substantial contribution to the age-old theological discourse on the Trinity in a fresh way. This invaluable treatise would make anyone think twice if they had doubts about what new insight could possibly be brought to this well-trodden path. It draws on the best of the available models, hermeneutics, and propositions from both the West and the East and combines these artistically with fresh insights from African Christianity and cosmology. A splendid work on the mystery of the Trinity and one of a kind from the African context – beautifully written and presented in ways both contextually relevant and doctrinally sound.

**Joseph Galgalo**
Associate Professor of Systematic Theology and Vice Chancellor
St Paul's University, Limuru, Kenya

The African church has been waiting for this book, and so have the rest of us who live outside Africa. James Kombo enters into a deep dialogue with the West and the East about the doctrine of the Trinity then proceeds to show us that "Christianity has more centers than two." He presents a fully African Trinitarian theology which rightly takes its place alongside historic Western and Eastern discussions. This is African *and* catholic theology at its best, offered for the well-being of the church in Africa and the rest. A must read for anyone anywhere who wants to understand and worship the glory of the Trinity.

**Gene L. Green**
Professor of New Testament
Wheaton College and Graduate School, Illinois, USA

James Kombo is one of the leading Protestant voices in contemporary African theology. Scholars, pastors, and theological students throughout the global church will benefit from this book's valuable contribution to understanding the doctrine of the Trinity. Covering a vast amount of theological and philosophical territory in remarkably clear and admirably succinct terms, Kombo clarifies alternative models of the Triune God and puts forward his own constructive proposal. It is a rare achievement – a robust, contextual, African theology of God as Trinity that emerges from deep within the classical Christian confession. This is an essential book for any student of World Christianity.

**Jeffrey P. Greenman**
President, Regent College, Vancouver, Canada

# Contents

Preface ........................................................................................................ix

Introduction ................................................................................................ 1
    The Beginning Point ............................................................................... 1
    Evangelical Formularies: The Problem of Language, New
        Developments, Faith Commitment and Secondary Theology ......... 2
    The Point of Departure .......................................................................... 6
    "Spoiling the Egyptians" ...................................................................... 12
    Flow of the Book and Summary of Chapters ..................................... 14
    Conclusion ........................................................................................... 18

Chapter 1 .................................................................................................. 21
    *Canons, Texts and Interpretations:*
    *Ideas of God among the Jews of Jesus' Day*
        1.1 Introduction ............................................................................... 21
        1.2 *Māšîaḥ* as an Interiorization of the God Relationship ............... 23
        1.3 Individuation of Wisdom ........................................................... 27
        1.4 The Preexistent Logos ................................................................ 30
        1.5 The Spirit of God ....................................................................... 31
        1.6 Conclusion ................................................................................. 33

Chapter 2 .................................................................................................. 37
    *Testimonies of the Early Church:*
    *Christian Identity, Theological Language and the Creeds*
        2.1 Introduction ............................................................................... 37
        2.2 Christian Identity: The Third Race Question ........................... 38
        2.3 Theological Language: Ousia, Hypostasis, Persona, Prosopon ..... 41
        2.4 The Creeds .................................................................................. 44
        2.5 Conclusion ................................................................................. 47

Chapter 3 .................................................................................................. 49
    *God as Essence*
        3.1 Platonism, Neo-Platonism, Aristotelianism and Theology .......... 49
        3.2 St Augustine: God as the Godhead ............................................ 50
        3.3 Boethius: God as the Divine Substance .................................... 54
        3.4 The Influence of Islam and Judaism: God as His Non-Divisible
            Essence ...................................................................................... 56

  3.5 Thomas Aquinas: God as His Essence ......................................... 58
  3.6 Conclusion ............................................................................... 62

## Chapter 4 ................................................................................. 65
### *God as Absolute Subject*
  4.1 Beginnings of Self-Consciousness........................................... 65
  4.2 Karl Barth ............................................................................... 70
    Self-Revelation ..................................................................... 70
    God as the Father ................................................................. 71
    The Son ................................................................................ 72
    The Holy Spirit .................................................................... 73
    Perichoresis ........................................................................... 73
  4.3 Karl Rahner ............................................................................. 74
    Self-Communication ........................................................... 74
    God as the Father ................................................................. 76
    The Son ................................................................................ 77
    The Holy Spirit .................................................................... 77
    Ordering the Modes ............................................................ 78
  4.4 Renown Theologians in the Model ........................................ 80
  4.5 Conclusion ............................................................................... 81

## Chapter 5 ................................................................................. 83
### *God as Community in Unity*
  5.1 Apophaticism ........................................................................... 83
  5.2 The Divine Energies ................................................................ 85
  5.3 God as Father, Son and Holy Spirit ........................................ 87
  5.4 Hypostases Exist in *Perichoresis* ............................................. 89
  5.5 The Filioquism versus Monopatrism ..................................... 90
  5.6 The Father as *Monarkhia* ........................................................ 92
  5.7 Renown Theologians in the Model ........................................ 93
  5.8 Conclusion ............................................................................... 96

## Chapter 6 ................................................................................. 97
### *God as Nyasaye*
  6.1 The Great Distractions: Tylor's Animism and Missionary
    Theologizing ......................................................................... 97
  6.2 The Access: Ubuntu Philosophy ........................................... 100
  6.3 The Trinitarian Moment ....................................................... 105
  6.4 The Father: The Divine *Monarchia* ...................................... 110
  6.5 The Holy Spirit ...................................................................... 112

  6.6 The Son ........................................................................................114
    Solution to Transcendence-Immanence Question ....................115
    Relationship with the Son as a Matter of Life and Death .........118
  6.7 Conclusion ..................................................................................120

Bibliography................................................................................... 123

Index............................................................................................... 133

# Preface

In the nine years since I published *The Doctrine of God in African Christian Thought: The Holy Trinity, Theological Hermeneutics and the African Intellectual Culture* (2007), I have fostered a good deal of interest in developing a full Systematic Theology. This book in my opinion is a first step towards a bigger project of Systematic Theology that is molded along the contours of the African worldview, a conception of doctrine which challenges existing patterns of theological reflection, a theology that has fully paid attention to global voices, and a theology which is as thoroughly evangelical as it is *fides quaerens intellectum*.

While by offering this book for publication I set out to realize some of these initial objectives, I am aware that the book itself is just the beginning of a bigger project which I intend to complete later with God's help. However, in stepping out I am happy I have joined the other worthy voices in the bigger field of Global Theology. I want to particularly thank Professor Jeff Greenman, the president of Regent College, who as the Dean of School of Theology at Wheaton College had earlier on identified the thrust of Global Theology for his doctoral students, and sought my expertise as an invited guest professor at the School of Theology, Wheaton College, in the spring of 2009. By this gesture, Professor Greenman gave me a privileged platform, an environment, and the much needed resources which facilitated the embryonic conversations that would mature into the present book. Professor Greenman, thank you.

In completing this work, my family encouraged me and sat with me for long hours into the night – much appreciation to my wife Pamela, daughter Leonida, and sons Philip and Samuel. I also acknowledge my parents Leonida and Paul Kombo, who raised me in a creedal church, and my mother-in-law and father-in-law, Lois and Philip, who have never ceased to pray for me.

*Soli Deo Gloria!*

# Introduction

## The Beginning Point

God in the Christian faith is viewed within the perplexity of unity and plurality: the Father is God, the Son is God, and the Holy Spirit is God, yet not three gods nor a monad in the sense of the Greek philosophers' description of God, but one God worshiped in the Trinity. Trinitarian scholarship indicates that in the development of the doctrine of God as we know it today, the theological questions that dominated the Christian consciousness from the very early stages were: (1) "Is the divine that has appeared on earth and reunited man with God identical with the supreme divine, which rules heaven and earth, or is it a demigod?"[1] (2) How does this divine relate to the Holy Spirit?[2] In offering an account to these questions, the Early Church saw God as three and one at the same time. C. F. H. Henry explains that if this understanding of God was to be reduced to a mathematical formula, it would probably be 3x in 1y and not 3x = 1x as presumed in some quarters.[3]

---

1. J. Pelikan, *The Christian Tradition*, vol. I (Chicago: The University of Chicago Press, 1971), 172–175.

2. Ibid., 213–215.

3. C. F. H. Henry, *God, Revelation and Authority, Vol V: God Who Stands and Stays Part One* (Waco, TX: World Book Publishing House, 1982), 165.

# Evangelical Formularies: The Problem of Language, New Developments, Faith Commitment and Secondary Theology

The excerpt below offers what could be a stinging criticism to the doctrine of the Trinity on the ground of the problem of language, modern developments, faith commitment and secondary theology. C. Hall, representing the critics of the doctrine, has the following explanation:

> The Trinity is the great unknown. The Trinity, to use a familiar equation, is viewed as a riddle wrapped up inside a puzzle and buried in an enigma. A riddle for how can any entity be at the same time multiple (three) yet singular (one)? A puzzle for the Trinity is so clearly contrary to any rational thought as not to warrant a second thought from sensible people. An enigma, for even if the Trinity could be understood, of what practical value, even what religious value, would it have for ordinary people?[4]

In their different ways, the critics of the doctrine of the Trinity dismiss it as "the most enigmatic Christian doctrine."[5] Others think it is "a mathematical monstrosity,"[6] while still others are of the conviction that it is "the most brutal and inexcusable error in counting."[7]

Note however that the problem of language is not limited to the doctrine of the Trinity. It extends to all our speech about God. Elizabeth Johnson has developed what she sees as the three ground rules that govern all speech about God: (1) that the reality of God comes through as a mystery beyond all imagining, incomprehensible and incapable of being wrapped in the net of our concepts since the idea itself is remote and transcendent from ordinary thought; (2) that whether explained by a theory of analogy, metaphor, or symbol, all human words about the divine proceed by way of indirection – our understanding and speech about God is indirect; and (3) that there

---

4. C. Hall, "Adding up Trinity," *Christianity Today* (28 April 1997): 26.
5. Ibid., 26–28.
6. Henry, *God, Revelation and Authority*, 165.
7. K. E. Yandell, "The Most Brutal and Inexcusable Error in Counting: Trinity and Consistency," *Religious Studies* 30 (1994): 201–217.

must be many names for God – God in the Bible is thus intended by the convergence of numerous and partial discourses (narrative, prophecy, command, wisdom writings, and hymns of celebration and lament), despite this polyphony of discourse, he is still a reality that eludes them all.[8]

In the context of this initial setback, we still have to find a way of relating theology to language. Thomas McPherson offers four levels of responses as he sees them in the field of theology. He states the responses as follows: (1) the Christian doctrines in general and the doctrine of the Trinity in particular have absurdities or paradoxes that cannot simply be expressed by language; (2) what is really important is Christian life – the Christians and theologians, according to this opinion, are exhorted to be as children and to stop worrying about the absurdities and paradoxes; (3) the doctrine of the Trinity like other Christian doctrines has difficulties with human language, however, sense can be made of them if we allow for the analogical language (that is words whose meanings are derived from their application to finite things in everyday speech); and (4) that there is no point in trying to express the inexpressible[9] – in other words, let's forget about the doctrine of the Trinity as it is inexpressible.

Response (3) above is most preferred in the field of evangelical theology. The basic argument for its preferential treatment is the view that speakers of all languages have different ways of speaking that is dependent on what may be obligatory or appropriate. Theological language is thus a vehicle of analogical reference. In itself, the language is radically unlike God who is its extralinguistic object. The language, even mother tongue in the case of indigenous Africa, in attempting to articulate the idea of God is made to transcend itself and to attain adequacy to its object. Thus theological language by analogy could be said to be truly referring to God in all his reality. Put in the words of Daniel Hardy, ". . . there is an actual correspondence

---

8. Elizabeth A. Johnson, "Naming God She: The Theological Implications," Boardman Lecture XXXVII (Centennial Lecture), Department of Religious Studies, University of Pennsylvania, presented on 19 October 2000.

9. Thomas McPherson, "Positivism and Religion," in *Religious Language and the Problem of Religious Knowledge*, ed. R. E. Santoni (Bloomington: Indiana University Press, 1968).

between reality and thought or language if the thinker is conformed to the mode of rationality afforded by reality."[10]

Note also that the doctrine of the Trinity has in addition been assessed on the ground of developments and sets of categories that it was never about in its right historical and textual context. For instance, the doctrine of the Trinity was never about language and logic, and neither was it about mathematics or the disciplines that we cherish so much in our own time. The doctrine of the Trinity was about the mystery God who had revealed himself in the Son and in the Holy Spirit. St Basil, one of the Cappadocian Fathers who labored so hard on the wording of the Trinitarian formula, offers this freeing response:

> In delivering the formula of the Father, the Son, and the Holy Ghost, Matthew 28:19, our Lord did not connect the gift with number. He did not say into First, Second, and Third, nor yet into one, two, and three, but He gave us the boon of the knowledge of the faith which leads to salvation, by means of holy names. So that what saves us is our faith. Number has been devised as a symbol indicative of the quantity of objects. But these men, who bring ruin on themselves from every possible source, have turned even the capacity for counting against the faith. Nothing else undergoes any change in consequence of the addition of number, and yet these men in the case of the divine nature pay reverence to number, lest they should exceed the limits of the honour due to the Paraclete. But, O wisest sirs, let the unapproachable be altogether above and beyond number, as the ancient reverence of the Hebrews wrote the unutterable name of God in peculiar characters, thus endeavouring to set forth its infinite excellence. Count, if you must; but you must not by counting do damage to the faith. Either let the ineffable be honoured by silence; or let holy things be counted consistently with true religion. There is one God and Father, one Only-begotten, and one Holy

---

10. Daniel W. Hardy, "Created and Redeemed Society," in *On Being the Church: Essays on the Christian Community*, eds. Colin E. Gunton and Daniel W. Hardy (Edinburgh: T&T Clark, 1989), 77.

Ghost. We proclaim each of the hypostases singly; and, when count we must, we do not let an ignorant arithmetic carry us away to the idea of a plurality of Gods.

For we do not count by way of addition, gradually making increase from unity to multitude, and saying one, two, and three, – nor yet first, second, and third.[11]

Samuel Miller sees the people engaged in ridiculing the formulary as those "who have either far departed or at least begun to depart, from the faith once delivered to the saints." For Miller the reason such people reject the evangelical definitions is because they are in the first place enemies of the Redeemer. For him, nobody will be "opposed to creeds, until creeds have become opposed to them."[12] S. McFague supports this position and sees it as a predominantly Western problem. He explains that in the context of Western society, the challenge persists because society is first and foremost unsure about God and then it is only secondarily unsure of its language about God. For McFague as for Miller the problem of the religious language originates at the experiential level and soon it spreads to the expressive level.[13]

In discussing the Trinity, there is also the temptation to think that the real matter is secondary theology. Those who come from this position see the discourse as concerned fundamentally with discussing what other theologians such as Augustine, Boethius, Aquinas, Calvin and so on said about God. In other words, the doctrine of the Trinity is about the ideas of the church fathers and their faithful descendants. There is a sense in which this way of conversation entrenches theological hegemony and for the nonwestern world in particular, sees the doctrine of the Trinity as attempts to recapture for that context the thoughts of previous western theologians such as Augustine, Boethius, Aquinas, Calvin. Theology, nevertheless, must be a primary discourse about God whom we have come to know in Christ

---

11. St Basil of Caesarea, *De Spiritu Sancto*, chapter 18, 44, 45. Downloaded on 7 May 2009 at http://www.newadvent.org/fathers/3203.htm.

12. S. Miller, "The Utility and Importance of Creeds and Confessions," in *Doctrinal Integrity: On the Utility and Importance of Creeds and Confessions and Adherence to Our Doctrinal Standards*, ed. S. Miller (Dallas: Presbyterian Heritage Publications, 1989), 25.

13. S. McFague, *Metaphorical Theology* (London: SCM Press, 1983), 1–4.

and worship in the Spirit. Indeed this debate opens us up to the rich theological conversation around the *Grundaxiom* and how we are to win it for our context.

## The Point of Departure

Why another book on the Trinity?

The doctrine of the Trinity is the foundational doctrine for Christian theology, doxology and practice. Indeed as T. F. Torrance says, the Trinity is "the innermost heart of the Christian faith, the central dogma of classical theology, [and] the fundamental grammar of our knowledge of God."[14] This means therefore that there cannot be enough discourses on the doctrine of the Trinity. The irony however is that there isn't much thought on the Trinity presented in the form in which this volume is done and neither are there contributions of this width and magnitude from the African Christian community which is the primary audience of the present work. Discourses on the Trinity have appeared to be the affair of the Northern continents: the Western side of the story representing Europe and North America and the Eastern side representing Eastern Europe and Russia. Whereas there have been historical and pragmatic reasons for this, the rise to significance of the global south, Africa in particular, on the Christian map in the recent history must mean that from now on the global south, Africa included, must be around the table.

This book sees intellectual culture as a theological hermeneutic. It recalls the prominence of "Spoiling the Egyptian" in primary theologizing as a tool for incarnating the gospel in the receiving contexts. Moreover the presentation of the doctrine in terms of the models provides a combination of both primary and secondary accounts of God all in the same text. The models are put next to each other thus making easy the possibility of comparison, contrast and analysis. The proximity to each other also symbolizes the unfinished task considering the potential models that could emerge given the variety of dominant intellectual cultures particularly in the global south. The table on the following page shows the models the current work espouses:

---

14. T. F. Torrance, *The Trinitarian Perspective: Toward Doctrinal Agreement* (Edinburgh: T&T Clark, 1994), 1.

| God as Essence | God as Absolute Subject | God as Community in Unity | God as Great Muntu |
|---|---|---|---|
| Neo-Platonism-Aristotellianism | German Idealism | Apophaticism – doxology | Ubuntu Philosophy |
| Begins with the One and then figures out the how of the Three | Begins with the One and figures out the how of the Three | Begins with the Three and figures out the how of the One | Begins with the Three and figures out the how of the One |
| God as the substance that is common to the hypostases | God as the Father | God as the Father | God as the Father |
| Deo Uno and Deo Trinitate dualistically presented | Economic Trinity as Immanent Trinity and vice versa | Economic Trinity not Immanent Trinity | Economic Trinity as immanent Trinity and vice versa |
| Hypostases as masks and the real actor is the One | Hypostases are portrayed as modes | The Three hypostases in the Scripture are dominant and exist in a perichoretic relationship | The Three hypostases in the Scripture are dominant and exist in a perichoretic relationship |
| Teaches *filioque* | Rahnerian side of the model not very favorable to *filioque* | Rejects *filioque* on account of logic for *monopatrism* | Teaches *filioque* |
| Favorable to vestiges of the Trinity | Barthians view Trinity discourse as necessitated by *fides quarens intellectum* while the Rahnarians are more favorable to vestiges of the Trinity | Divine energies and *theosis* are together an important part of the Trinity discourse | The Trinity discourse as necessitated by *fides quarens intellectum* |

**Table 1**

The book notices the relationship between the intellectual infrastructure of the receiving culture and the model of the doctrine of the Trinity the culture shapes for itself. It posits the view that the models indicate clear differences from each other not on account of the biblical factor but on account of respective dominant intellectual culture, which shapes ways of speaking and filters what may be obligatory or appropriate in its receiving culture. This way, the study reinforces the now well-understood idea of the contextuality of all theology and the concomitant translatability of the Christian faith. It also recognizes that the models of theology determine whether the focus is primarily the academia or the doxological, a primary discourse on God or secondary discourses on what others think of God. The fact that the models are so different and represent a wide geographical divide and demographic interests, yet they all appear to have paid adequate attention to biblical testimony, is perhaps an indication that none of the models is adequate in itself and that all of them are in fact necessary.

But the doctrine of the Trinity has another significance to theological discourse – it functions as a theological hermeneutic. In the context of the ever-growing Christianity in the global South, for instance, proper *theologia* must concern itself primarily with who God is even as we engage in evangelization, incarnation of the faith into indigenous cosmology, and interreligious dialogue. We are then able to speak of God's rule in every area of the cosmology. This way, theology is not compartmentalized into liberation, inculturation, womanist/feminist and so on as in Africa today; instead all these areas are seen as the arena of the rule of God. Such a theology cannot avoid but be *fides quarens intellectum*. This kind of theology focuses on speaking about the God we have come to know through the ministry of Jesus who is the revelation of the Father who's rule we experience.

African theology for instance has since the 1970s witnessed some of the most bruising theological battles on the standing of the African traditional religions versus Christianity. In this case, theology appears to have allowed itself to be a secondary conversation and not a primary discourse about the God we have come to know in Christ and worship in the Holy Spirit. Consequently, theology in Africa for many decades joined the battle on a foreign ground and the consequences have been less than optimistic. As a result of this clash, one notes roughly four distinct responses complete with followership. (1) The view that the African traditional religions had no or only distorted revelation and no salvation. This position is articulated mainly by Byang Kato and Tokunboh Adeyemo.[15] (2) The second approach allows for revelation but rejects any possibility for salvation. John S. Mbiti and Charles Nyamiti are the serious proponents of this view.[16] (3) The third group argues for both revelation and salvation in African traditional religion, *but* they also insist that the highest revelation and salvation are only in the Christian faith. The proponents of this are Patrick Kalilombe and Laurenti Magesa.[17] (4) The final group argues that there is indeed revelation and salvation in African traditional religions, thus allowing for no "but." For this position, all religions are unique and relative ways of salvation. Among the proponents of this view are Samuel Kibicho, Anatole Byaruhanga-Akiiki and Okot p'Bitek.[18]

Whereas African theology can now not evade the debate it allowed itself to be drawn into, at least it can change the paradigm of discourse and ask

---

15. Byang Kato, *Biblical Christianity in Africa* (Achimota, Ghana: Africa Christian Press, 1985), 11; see also his *Theological Pitfalls* (Kisumu, Kenya: Evangel Publishing House, 1975), 16; Tokunboh Adeyemo, *Salvation in an African Tradition* (Nairobi: Evangel Publishing House, 1979), 96; see also his article "The Salvation Debate and Evangelical Response," *East African Journal of Evangelical Theology* 2 (1984): 4–19.

16. Charles Nyamiti, *African Tradition and the Christian God* (Eldoret: Gaba Publications, 1979); see also his *The Way to Christian Theology for Africa* (Eldoret: Gaba Publications, 1978). For John S. Mbiti's line of thought see his "Our Savior as an African Experience," in *Christ and Spirit in the New Testament*, eds. B. Lindars, S. Smalley, and C. F. D. Moule (Cambridge: Cambridge University Press, 1973), 397–414; and his other work "Some Reflections on the African Experience of Salvation Today," in *Living Faiths and Ultimate Goals: A Continuing Dialogue*, ed. S. J. Samartha (Geneva: WCC, 1974), 108–119.

17. Patrick Kalilombe, "Evangelization and the Holy Spirit," *African Ecclesial Review* 18 (1976): 8–18; also his article "The Salvific Value of the African Religions," *African Ecclesial Review* 21 (1979): 143–156. Laurenti Magesa, "Evangelisation," *African Ecclesial Review* (1982): 354–362; and "Who are 'the People of God'?" *African Ecclesial Review* 26 (1984): 204–212.

18. Samuel Kibicho, "The Teaching of African Religion in our Schools and Colleges and the Christian Attitude towards this Religion," *Africa Theological Journal* 10 (1981): 3, 29–37; see also his "Revelation in African Religion," *Africa Theological Journal* 12 (1983): 3, 166–177. A. Byaruhanga-Akiiki, "Spirituality in African Traditions," BOLESWA Occassional Papers on Theology and Religion, Number 1 (University of Botswana, Lesotho and Swaziland, 1988); see also his work "African Traditional Values for Human Development," in *Church Contributions to Integral Development*, eds. Deogratias M. Byabazaire, Joseph Thérèse Agbasiere, and Boniface K. Zabajungu (Eldoret: Gaba Publications, 1989), 45–62. See also Okot p'Bitek, *African Religions in Western Scholarship* (Nairobi: Kenya Literature Bureau, 1970).

questions that it sees as significant to its cause. This change of paradigm must involve at least two things: (1) the recognition of the mother tongues and indigenous intellectual cultures as capable of transcending themselves and to attain adequacy to truly express God in all his reality; and (2) the movement of theology to the plane of a primary discourse on God who has called us in Christ and to see secondary engagements as essential conversations done out of the necessity to interact.

The use of non-Western languages in mainstream theology is a new thing. This has arisen not only because of logic for translation of the Bible into vernaculars and the pragmatic issue of worship in these languages but more fundamentally because these languages are themselves living languages. The basic argument here is that the non-Western languages too are theological languages. A typical example of the wrong way to go is seen in sections of the works of Andrew Lang quoted below:

> The phrases "Creator," "creative," as applied to Anyambi, or Baime, have been described, by critics, as rhetorical, covertly introducing conceptions of which savages are incapable. I have already shown that I only follow my authorities, and their translations of phrases in various savage tongues. But the phrase "eternal" applied to Anyambi or Baime, may be misleading. I do not wish to assert that, if you talked to a savage about "eternity," he would understand what you intend.
>
> With these explanations I trust that my rhetorical use of such phrases as "eternal," "creative," "omniscient," "omnipotent," "omnipresent," and "moral" may not be found to mislead or covertly import modern or Christian ideas into my account of the religious conceptions of savages.[19]

Others like Eric Waterhouse follow the same trend. They roundly condemn those they think have "illegitimately" used Christian theological terms to describe the concepts of the Supreme Being among the peoples they consider primitives.[20] Charles E. Fuller, writing from the same point of view, suggests that "weighted terms such as omnipotence, omniscience,

---

19. A. Lang, *The Making of Religion* (London: Longmans, 1898), xxii–xxiv.
20. B. Idowu, *Olódùmarè: God in Yoruba Belief* (London: Longmans, 1962), 3.

and eternity are . . . too interlaced with theological complexities of the traditions common to Jewish, Moslem, and Christian faiths to be used in any neutral sense when observing religions external to these."²¹ Fuller goes so far as to suggest that in the African context, we should instead "speak of 'divinity' where reference is made to 'god' or 'gods.'"²²

With Karl Barth, I embrace the position that "every theological statement is an inadequate expression of its object." This is regardless of the language in which the statement comes: whether English or French, Luo or Kiswahili. Every understanding of God in whatever language it is framed is ultimately inadequate. Indeed as Barth argues: "Strictly speaking, it is only God himself who has a conception of God. All that we have are conceptions of objects, none of which is identical with God." The theologian is here reminded that "God shutters every syllogism." This is not to over approximate the vernaculars and neither is this to say that theology is an impossibility. The point is that it is only God who can make human language, regardless of its standing in the human society, adequate for purposes of theology: "Just as everything which is not God could not exist apart from God and is something only because of God, so it is possible for expressions which are really appropriate to objects that are not identical with God to be true expressions."²³

Primary articulations on God, on the other hand, provide patterns with which we can incarnate the Christian content into the African cosmology thereby address the totality of the African cosmology: God; sprits, divinities, ancestors; humankind; animals and plants; and objects without biological life. Theology is yet to deal with these areas – most importantly God, the ancestors, the divinities and the spirits – for purposes of effective evangelization. Thus in the case of Africa, the clashes as well as the need to reconfigure the cosmology are reasons serious enough to warrant a call for another way of carrying out theological discourse.

---

21. C. E. Fuller, "God in African Thought and Life," in *God in Contemporary Thought: A Philosophical Perspective*, ed. S. Matczak (New York: Learned Publications, 1977), 20.

22. Ibid., 21.

23. Karl Barth, *Fides Quarens Intellectum. Anselm's Proof of the Existence of God in the Context of His Theological Scheme*, trans. Ian W. Robertson (London: SCM Press, 1960), 29.

The Trinitarian hermeneutic has what it takes to incarnate biblical cosmology into the African cosmology and to cast the entire theological discourse on a completely different plane. Indeed, Karl Barth, faced with a similar situation, found the Trinitarian hermeneutic useful. The Divine understood from this point of view gives room for a heartfelt doxology and a high level primary discourse about the God the theologian has met in Christ. This is well put in the ancient dictum: *lex credendi, lex orandi; lex orandi, lex credendi* (the phrase literally means "how we worship reflects what we believe" and vice versa).

## "Spoiling the Egyptians"

The basis of intellectual culture as a theological hermeneutic is what theology has always known and implemented as "Spoiling the Egyptians." Each of the models discussed in this book appear to have attained identification by borrowing and appropriating the intellectual resources of target communities to formulate and deliver the doctrine of the Trinity. This appears to be the approach the church fathers found useful. Indeed as G. Ernest Wright explains, the early church borrowed and used frequently from the surrounding cultures:

> In general, it may be said that there was the greatest freedom in borrowing from the surrounding culture, and tension arose over such borrowing only when it threatened the basis of community faith or when its reinterpretation in biblical setting was too slow to keep pace with the deepening of insight into the implications of the faith.[24]

It is important to note that what the fathers borrowed from the target cultures was not the theological content or the existential realities. They were clear that they had content in the Christian faith. For instance, in the case of the Trinity, they did not have interest in the *theos* of Gnosticism since Yahweh of Israel had so clearly made himself known to them. They however had interest in borrowing the categories of speaking about *theos* where such would be useful in applying such imageries as gateways to

---

24. G. E. Wright, *The Biblical Doctrine of Man and Society* (London: SCM Ltd., 1954), 153.

Yahweh. All the models of the doctrine of the Trinity presented in this book have understood and implemented this perspective. In other words, the book senses that the respective proponents of the models took from the host cultures ordinary categories and patterns of thought to communicate the idea of God which was remote from ordinary thought.

In the context of the church fathers, it must be noted that borrowing from target cultures, also known as "Spoiling the Egyptians,"[25] was never a one-track affair nor was it a casual matter. For Augustine it was a stint with Manichaeism, study of other contemporary philosophies, and special fondness for Neo-Platonism.[26] Cyprian had a similar experience. His exposure as a tutor of rhetoric identified him with students of philosophy and reason.[27] Origen on his part was instructed in Neo-Platonism from the intellectual Ammonius Saccas.[28] He is also said to have had keen interest in this syncretistic form of Christianity to the extent that he spent much time studying Greek literature. He is known to have become a scholar in the field.[29] Clement brought into "Spoiling the Egyptians" his education in many cultures. He learned at the feet of teachers from various backgrounds including a Syrian, an Egyptian, an Assyrian, and a Palestinian Hebrew. He is also said to have learned from the stoics, especially those of Epictetus.[30] Both Clement and Origen used the debates in presenting the faith the same way as the philosophers.[31] Tertullian, Cyprian and Origen wrote extensively on how the Christian is to understand and deal with the evil spirits. This way, they corrected Gnosticism and "created" and incarnated into the Greek cosmology the Christian view of demons.[32] Tertullian is on record as having popularized Latin to attract his fellow Italians and to

---

25. M. Green, *Evangelism in the Early Church* (Grand Rapids, MI: Eerdmans, 1971), 19.

26. Kenneth Scott Latourette, *A History of the Expansion of Christianity*, vol. 1 (Grand Rapids: Zondervan Publishing House, 1970), 172; see also E. H. Broadbent, *The Pilgrim Church* (London: Pickering & Inglis Ltd., 1931), 24.

27. Latourette, *A History of the Expansion of Christianity*, 288.

28. Ibid., 20.

29. Eusebius Pamphilus, *Ecclesiastical History* (Grand Rapids, MI: Baker Book House, 1966), 219.

30. Latourette, *A History of the Expansion of Christianity*, 260.

31. Ibid., 249.

32. Green, *Evangelism in the Early Church*, 192.

promote their understanding of the gospel. Indeed his greatest contribution is his use of the word "trinity" for the relationship between the Father, Son and Holy Spirit.[33]

Whereas the church fathers valued the instruments of cultures of reception, it is important to state simultaneously that they did not approve of everything the receiving cultures were about. Indeed they remained critical to these cultures and saw themselves as first and foremost missionaries and change agents. For instance, they attacked specific practices and beliefs of the unsaved and sought to change such practices from their very core. The fathers believed that the new faith in Christ had shaken the very core of the world of the converts and therefore they needed to perceive and interact with their world in light of their new reality. This would mean a change of their cosmology from the inside. Tertullian condemned oath taking when borrowing money from pagans because it involved contact with the Greek gods.[34] Certain trades were also not acceptable for Christians because of their association with idolatry.[35] Christians were not to take part in war; therefore the non-Christians converting to Christianity had to quit the Roman army[36] and as a general rule, as Latourette notes, the Fathers were against such "spectacles like the circus, gladiatorial events, and the theater."[37]

## Flow of the Book and Summary of Chapters

This book is primarily a conversation with the different models of the Trinity identified. As such it is not intended to be a critique of any of the models. To develop its central thesis, the book takes a four-tiered framework. First, (chapter 1) I recognize and bring into the picture the active self-presentation of God known to us in Christ and worshiped in the Holy Spirit as the reality presented to us in the Scripture; second (chapter 2) I press deeper to understand how the early church responded to what they saw of God; third (chapters 3–5), I probe the responses of the church in

---

33. F. F. Bruce, *The Spreading Flame* (Exeter, England: The Paternoster Press, 1958), 256.
34. Latourette, *A History of the Expansion of Christianity*, 264.
35. Green, *Evangelism in the Early Church*, 47.
36. Bruce, *The Spreading Flame*, 181.
37. Latourette, *A History of the Expansion of Christianity*, 269–270.

its various traditions into what it has seen of God; and lastly (chapter 6), from this development and conversations, I present what I see as a plausible proposal for the African context.

Chapter 1: "Canon, Texts and Interpretations" takes the view that the Jews of Jesus' time were exposed to many canons and texts, and that these in turn were interpreted in many ways. This meant that in its own formation, Christianity had to adopt a particular canon, cling to the texts provided by the canon, and interpret the texts in a particular way. In deciding how to understand God, for instance, Christianity went to the canon and the texts they received from their Jewish heritage. In the texts they saw: (1) passages of identity which posit simple identity of Christ with God, (2) passages of distinction which distinguish one "lord" from another "lord," and (3) passages of derivation which suggest that the Son is from the Father. As they interacted with the texts, they came to see different perspectives of the following Old Testament ideas: the Messiah, Wisdom, the Logos, and the Spirit of God. They discovered in the texts the requirement of the belief that God became incarnate, suffered on the cross, and redeemed mankind by dying and rising again. In other words, for this Jewish group, God endured to be born, to become man, and to suffer thus a ground for an ητερος θεος. Here then was the emergence of a form of monotheism that was neither a Christian conspiracy nor secrecy. This conception of monotheism was often publicly celebrated and debated. Indeed it was an occasion for martyrdom for many and was demonstrated to have arisen from and therefore a requirement of the canons and the texts.

Chapter 2: "Testimonies of the Early Church" discusses the church's reaction to their own confession of the Lordship of Jesus Christ. The confession caused an identity crisis – for the first time they needed to know the nature of their corporate identity. This meant not only a break with Judaism but also internal struggles with what appeared to be heterodoxies and the eventual emergence of what was to become mainstream Christianity. The other part of the search for identity was the quest for theological language. The chapter shows that this was necessary on account of a cultural crossing from a Jewish world to the faith's new heartland. Thus the fathers, individually through their writings and ministries on the one hand and corporately through councils (Nicea-325, and Constantinople-381) on the other hand, agreed on formularies which naturally became the creeds of the church. The chapter shows that the bishops borrowed the theological language (*ousia, hypostasis, prosopon, persona*) from the surrounding cultures and used the language in a manner that shows that the language was a mere vehicle of an analogical reference which transcended itself and attained adequacy to name God.

Chapter 3: "God as Essence" offers a model of the Trinity which sees God as the common substance shared by the three personae. Some of the most influential names behind this model are St Augustine of Hippo (c.354–c.430), Anicius Manlius Severinus Boethius (c.480–c.525AD) and St Thomas Aquinas (1225–1274). The model demonstrates acquaintance with Neoplatonism. Indeed St Augustine believed that a Christian in good standing was also a Neoplatonist. Boethius lived at the transition between St Augustine and the Middle Ages which also marked the movement from Neoplatonism to Aristotelianism. He considered it his responsibility to re-package the doctrine of the Trinity in Aristotelian categories for his generation and beyond. Between Boethius and St Aquinas, the chapter discusses the flowering of Islamic civilization and the dominance of Aristotelianism. The chapter notes that these two, Islam and Aristotelianism, so influenced and solidified the doctrine Boethius bequeathed to the point, that by the time of St Aquinas, the Trinity had become a matter of philosophical discourse about the divine monad. This position has no framework for discussing *filioque* since what is common is the substance and not the Father. But perhaps the other contribution of this chapter is the unique framing typical of Aristotelian heritage seen particularly in St Aquinas' works according to which God is dualistically discussed as *De Deo Uno* (the Godhead as the nature common to the three persons) and *De Deo Trino* effectively separating immanent Trinity from economic Trinity and assigning the attributes to *De Deo Uno*.

Chapter 4: "God as Absolute Subject" unpacks what it sees as a model of the Trinity with a dominant subject divinity and the two hypostases discussed as modes. According to this model, God means the Father. The chapter puts together what it considers to be a synopsis of Karl Barth and Karl Rahner on the Trinity as best examples of this kind of discourse. Revelation is for Barth the defining term while communication is Rahner's.

The chapter demonstrates that "God as Absolute Subject" model appears to follow German idealism very closely. Indeed Barth is on record as having argued that idealism has a deeper affinity to theology than realism.[38] Consequently, it is able to give a picture of an absolute subject rather than "substance" or "essence," to drive the need to modify language from "persons" to "modes," and to free the discourse to embrace the *grundaxiom* "immanent Trinity is the economic Trinity and vice versa." The chapter argues that since this model relies heavily on the metaphysics of self-consciousness and therefore talks of the Son and the Spirit as "modes" rather than "hypostases," it doesn't speak eloquently and optimistically of *filioque*. The chapter also notes the difference of Karl Barth and Karl Rahner on the grace.

Chapter 5: "God as Community in Unity" focuses on the three hypostases and sees them as existing in unity – *perichoresis*. The chapter further argues that the proponents of the model see God as the Father because he is the *monarche*. In other words, there is no "substance" or "essence" behind the two hypostases except the Father. The model rejects *filioque* and suggests more grounding of the Holy Spirit in *theologia*. The chapter notes that the proponents of this model have relied heavily on *apophatic* (negative) rather than *kataphatic* (positive) forms of argumentation. Here, discourse on the Trinity is invited to use oriental imagery, poetry and rhetoric. Mystery of God is emphasized and the entire process of theologizing is seen not as belonging primarily in the academy but as part of the experience of *theosis*. With this is the discourse on divine energies. The implication therefore is that there can be no discourse on the Trinity without talking of the One, the Three and the divine energies.

Chapter 6: "God as *Nyasaye*" is this author's primary discourse on God. The chapter begins by emphasizing that the pre-Christian African experience of God has turned out to be the gate through which Yahweh has penetrated Africa. This, as the chapter argues, does not only mean that for Luo people who call God *Nyasaye,* and indeed the other African peoples, the Trinity must emerge from *Nyasaye, Nyambe, Nyame* and so on – as various African peoples call God – but also that the Son and the Holy Spirit are now constitutive in the identity of the name *Nyasaye*. In this case,

---

38. Gary J. Dorrien, *The Barthian Revolt in Modern Theology: Theology without Weapons* (Westminster: John Knox Press, 1999).

confession of one God (monotheism) is not in the "common substance" or "common essence" terms of the Greco-Roman heritage, nor in the "monotheism as one-ness, non-divisible essence" in Islam and Neoplatonism, nor as oneness in the sense of "absolute subject" in the philosophy of German idealism. This model reaches out to *Ubuntu* philosophy and sees in it categories useful for discourse on the Trinity. Consequently, the One is the Father named variously by different African peoples: *Nyasaye, Ngai, Mulungu* and so on. *Nyasaye*, for instance, has his category (*UTU*)[39] split between the Son and the Holy Spirit. The Father in this case is *Nyasaye* (God) who uniquely shares the Divine category (*UTU*) with the Son and the Holy Spirit in a perichoretic relationship.

## Conclusion

The variety of Trinitarian models presented in this book testify to the limitations of theological language and the reality of our cultural differences. Speaking of what I see as a Luo speaker (an African vernacular) and therefore bringing my own limitation into the discourse, I can say that the models are all about *Nyasaye* disclosed as Trinitarian in history. *Nyasaye* is the Luo name for God. The name *Nyasaye* in this case functions as a vehicle of analogical reference which consequently attains adequacy to God. I can then join everyone in the discourse by saying that for me, *Nyasaye* as he exists in himself is what the various models have tried to say in their own ways. In this case, I can with the same argument say that *Nyasaye* exists in Trinitarian in eternity. As such, *Nyasaye* is knowable in and to himself in the life of the Trinity and therefore he can be known by us. Through *Nyasaye's* act in history as Father, Son and Holy Spirit, theology has been able to show that *Nyasaye* in fact exists in that manner and not as a monad in the immanent Trinity. In other words, as the Father, Son and Holy Spirit reveal themselves within the economy of salvation, so the three hypostases exist in the ontological Trinity. T. F. Torrance presents the same argument in the following words:

---

39. *UTU* in its literal sense is about the "we-ness" for all people. It is the moral practice and theory of humanness in which all human beings are treated with dignity, respect, kindness and empathy. *UTU* in this context is the "we-ness for God."

It is precisely the ontological Trinity that God has made known to us in his self-giving and self-revealing as Father, Son and Holy Spirit in salvation history, and it is on the ontological Trinity that the evangelical nature of the economic Trinity entirely depends.[40]

And so *Nyasaye* as he is in himself is no different from whom he is in relation to salvation. Consequently what we come to know of *Nyasaye* revealed through his acts in redemptive history is *Nyasaye* as he is in himself.

---

40. Thomas F. Torrance, *The Christian Doctrine of God: One Being Three Persons* (Edinburgh: T & T Clark, 1996), 109.

CHAPTER 1

# Canons, Texts and Interpretations: Ideas of God among the Jews of Jesus' Day

## 1.1 Introduction

The Jewish people of Jesus' time lived in what was clearly a conglomeration of Jewish sects, Hellenistic Roman religions, and Hellenistic Roman philosophies, all of which sought attention. Indeed this was a market place of Greek mysteries and Eastern religions such as Eleusinian mysteries; Dionysiac mysteries; Egyptian, Persian, Phoenician as well as Phrygian deities and Gnosticism. The Hellenist Roman philosophies in circulation included skepticism, cynicism and popular philosophy, Stoicism, Epicureanism, Eclectism, Neopythagoreanism, middle Platonism and Neoplatonism. The Jerusalem Talmud, according to Louis H. Feldman, identifies twenty-four Jewish sects at the time of the destruction of the Temple. Out of these, eight are commonly in the limelight: the Pharisees, the Sadducees, the Essenes, the "Fourth Philosophy," the ascetic Therapeutae, Herodians, the Samaritans, and the Christians.[1] The Pharisees, the Sadducees, the "Fourth Philosophy" and the Samaritans are classified as part of the group with radical messianism which made egalitarian and mass appeal. Then the Essenes, the Therapeutae, the Dead Sea sect and to an extent, Christianity, were

---

1. Everett Ferguson, *Backgrounds of Early Christianity* (Grand Rapids, MI: Eerdmans, 1987); see also Louis H. Feldman, "Palestinian and Diaspora Judaism in the First Century," in *Christianity and Rabbinic Judaism: A Parallel History of Their Origins and Early Development*, ed. Hershel Shanks (Washington, DC: Biblical Archeology Society, 1992), 12.

part of the other group which was classified as "separatists, utopian, ascetic, esoteric and preoccupied with ethics."[2]

Religious literature in circulation, and therefore authorities which are important in deciphering doctrine and practice at the time, included the Old Testament in Greek, versions of the Old Testament, Old Testament Apocrypha, Old Testament Pseudepigrapha, Dead Sea scrolls, accounts of Philo and Josephus, the New Testament, Rabbinic literature, the Targums, the New Testament Apocrypha and Pseudepigrapha, the early church fathers and the Gnostic writings.[3] The sects didn't always agree on the canon, authority of texts or the right interpretation. The Sadducees, for instance, on account of their rejection of the oral Torah which was critical in the formation of Pharisaic thinking supported Jewish nationalism. They read the Torah, which is what they accepted as the "canon" in a manner that necessitated that they take a restorative approach and thereby construct logic for Jewish nationalism. The "Fourth Philosophy," also on the basis of the authority of the "canon" they accepted and their interpretation of the Torah, were fiercely militant, restorative and overly critical of Pax Romana. They "refused to pay tribute to the Romans; they advocated rebellion on the ground that they could acknowledge only God as their master."[4] The Essenes and the Dead Sea sect regarded the "Temple Scroll" – which differs in some way from the Masoretic texts, the Septuagint and the Samaritan Pentateuch – as the original Torah. The Essenes agree with the Sadducees in some areas on the basis of their reading of the MMT.[5]

The sects mentioned here are Jewish sects. All of them were active at the time of Christ. They knew the God of Israel but they clearly did not have homogeneity on specific details. They did not always have the same texts. Moreover the canons they used varied from one group to another.

---

2. Feldman, "Palestinian and Diaspora Judaism," 13.

3. For detailed study on texts at the time of Christ see Craig A. Evans, *Ancient Texts for New Testament Studies: A Guide to the Background Literature* (Peabody, Massachusetts: Hendrickson Publishers), 2005.

4. Feldman, "Palestinian and Diaspora Judaism," 16.

5. This refers to Works of the Law which is a body of writings extant in the first century, the *Miqsat Ma'ase Ha-Torah* or *MMT*, which have only recently been recovered. Textual critics argue that the writings make Paul more intelligible to modern Christians as Works of the Law is explained in view of the more recent archaeological evidence using the Dead Sea Scrolls.

The texts and the canons in their varieties sustained the belief in Yahweh as Lord while at the same time pontificated about the Messiah who was to come, indicated a hypostasised wisdom, individuated the Spirit of God and had a heightened sense of the pre-existent Logos. In other words, by these characterizations the scriptural texts and the canons in circulation at the time of Jesus appeared to indicate a mystery God who begged to be understood as one and many simultaneously. Other sects could choose to ignore if not oppose what seemed to be the clear teaching of the Scripture. However what emerged as the mainstream Christianity appears to have had a determinative hermeneutic which shaped their interpretation of the scriptural texts, controlled what they understood to be the "canon" and altogether directed their understanding of the God of Israel.

## 1.2 *Māšîah* as an Interiorization of the God Relationship

Messianism appears to be the most contested christological handle in our time. Many believe the Christian scholars constructed the so-called "Messianic hope" of the Jews and imposed specificity in what was otherwise a general Jewish national hope which didn't have to entail a personal Messiah as the agent for bringing about the good tidings.[6] This criticism however forgets the fact that the Christians were themselves part of the Jewish community well informed by the abundance of literature in their midst as well as oral traditions on the one hand and by their hope and their understanding of the Messiah as a personal agent on the other hand. Indeed along with other Jewish sects, the Christians were aware of the earliest Jewish literature which linked David to Messianism at the very beginning of the emergence of royal ideology which encapsulates the ideals of Israelite kingship.[7] Through Nathan, God promised David:

> When your days are fulfilled and you lie down with your fathers, I will raise up your offspring after you, who shall come

---

6. See Ferguson, *Backgrounds of Early Christianity*, 437.

7. A. Laato, *A Star Is Rising: The Historical Development of the Old Testament Royal Ideology and the Rise of the Jewish Messianic Expectations*, USF International Studies in Formative Christianity and Judaism, 5 (Atlanta: Scholars Press, 1997), 4.

forth from your body, and I will establish his kingdom. ¹³He shall build a house for my name, and I will establish the throne of his kingdom for ever. ¹⁴I will be his father, and he shall be my son. When he commits iniquity, I will chasten him with the rod of men, with the stripes of the sons of men; ¹⁵but I will not take my steadfast love from him, as I took it from Saul, whom I put away from before you. ¹⁶And your house and your kingdom shall be made sure for ever before me; your throne shall be established for ever. (RSV: 2 Sam 7:12–16)

This prophecy offers what became the "messianic paradigm" across the board. From this point on, while the people will continue to anticipate a glorious destiny for Israel, they had a certain set of expectations of a Davidic descendant: he will build the temple, God will establish the throne of his kingdom forever, God will be his Father, while he will be God's son. Whereas Psalm 2 and 89 appeared to enhance this covenant, the prophets generally gave it eschatological dimensions. The pre-exilic prophets in particular offered ground for eschatological messianism (Hos 3:4–5; Mic 5:2; Isa 9:1–7; 11:1–5; 32:1) while they at the same time appeared to espouse radical as opposed to conservative views (Jer 30:8–9; Ezek 34:23–24; 37:24–25) holding in balance the twin idea of kingly and priestly messiah (Hag 1:12–14; 2:2–4 ; 2:20–23; Zech 3:6–10; 4:2–5; 4:11–14).

By the intertestamental period, the Jewish people appear to have had an expectation of the coming of a divinely anointed and empowered figure who would have no successor and who would inaugurate something dramatically new as opposed simply to the hope of restoring Israel's king. This idea is already available in Daniel 12 and Ezra 4. This period also ushers in diversity of messianic expectations.[8] Some of the messianisms at the time include, but are not limited to, what we see in the *Wisdom of Jesus Ben Sira* or *Ecclesiasticus* (c. 180 BCE). In reference to David, Sir 47:11 reads "The

---

8. For further reading, see W. Horbury, *Jewish Messianism and the Cult of the Christ* (London: SCM Press, 1998); and his other book, *Messianism among Jews and Christians: Twelve Biblical and Historical Studies* (London and New York: T. & T. Clark International, 2003). The other useful references are J. Neusner, W. S. Green, and E. S. Frerichs, eds., *Judaisms and their Messiahs at the Turn of the Christian Era* (Cambridge: Cambridge University Press, 1987); J. H. Charlesworth, ed., *The Messiah: Developments in Earliest Judaism and Christianity* (Minneapolis: Fortress Press, 1992).

Lord took away his sins, and exalted his power for ever; he gave him the covenant of kings and a throne of glory in Israel." Here we see a clear reference to the messianic covenant of 2 Samuel 7. Another reference is *Psalms of Solomon* 17 which talks of "their king is the Lord Messiah" who will denounce and eliminate ungodliness. The *Testaments of the Twelve Patriarchs* depicts priestly and royal figures as having messianic presentations while the *Similitudes of Enoch* has several references to the "son of man," the "chosen one," and two references to "Messiah" (48:10; 52:4). The messianic texts of Qumran Jews also talk of a "Messiah, whom heaven and earth will obey." It also suggests a link between the coming of the Messiah and the coming of the High Priest.

At the time of Christ, history records actual instances of attempts to fulfill the messianic prophecies. Josephus talks of:

> But what more than all else incited them to the war was an ambiguous oracle, likewise found in their sacred scriptures, to the effect that at that time one from their country would become ruler of the world. This they understood to mean someone of their own race, and many of their wise men went astray in their interpretation of it. The oracle, however, in reality signified the sovereignty of Vespasian, who was proclaimed Emperor on Jewish soil.[9]

This was the rebellion against Rome (c. 66 CE) which could have featured two insurgents: Menahem the son or grandson of Judas the Galilean, or Simon bar Giora. Whoever it was, Josephus thought he must have been a messiah; thus Josephus' connection of this particular messianic agent with the readings of Genesis 49:10 ("the scepter shall not depart from Judah") and numbers Numbers 24:17 ("a star [LXX: a stron] shall come forth out of Jacob, and a scepter shall rise out of Israel"). In the mind of Josephus, the incident must have been an implementation of a form of messianism, which presented the inauguration of a world ruler. In his

---

9. H. Thackeray, trans., *Josephus III*, The Loeb Classical Library series, 210 (London: Heinemann; Cambridge, MA: Harvard University Press, 1928), 467.

first *Apology*, Justin Martyr thinks the messiah Josephus talked about was Simon ben Kosiba.[10]

It appears that at some point, Christianity's perspective of the messiah they expected was going to be determinative of their continued existence in Judaism and all the other sects would also see this as their point of departure. The Pharisees crystallized a conservative messianism that was pro *Pax Romana*. The Sadducees, the "Fourth Philosophy," and the Samaritans appear to have settled for radical restorative and egalitarian forms of messianism thus clashes with the *status quo*. Other ascetic sects appear to have accepted utopian and moral laden messianism.[11] It is on record that Jewish messianism of the intertestamental period and the first two centuries of the Common Era posed a real threat to the Roman order as seen in the catastrophic rebellions that occurred in three successive generations: 66–70 CE, 115–116 CE and 132–135 CE. Every sect appears to have crystallized messianism into "something." In this mix of things, I would argue that it was perfectly legitimate for the Christians to solidify their messianism on the basis of well-formed opinion into what Scholem has described as "an interiorization of the God relationship and thereby as an individualization of the idea of the Messiah."[12]

Christianity, however in view of the significance of Christ, put together the proclamation of the reign of God (Mark 1:14–15; Luke 11:20), the high priesthood of Christ (Heb 2:17, 9:11–14, 10:5–12), Jesus' prediction

---

10. See discussions on whether Simon ben Kosiba was considered a messiah by his contemporaries: B. Isaac and A. Oppenheimer, "The Revolt of Bar Kokhba: Ideology and Modern Scholarship," *Journal of Jewish Studies* 36, no. 1 (1985): 33–60; A. Reinhartz, "Rabbinic Perceptions of Simeon bar Kosiba," *Journal for the Study of Judaism* 20, no. 2 (1989): 171–194; C. A. Evans, "Was Simon ben Kosiba Recognized as Messiah?," in *Jesus and his Contemporaries: Comparative Studies*, ed. C. A. Evans (Leiden: Brill, 1995), 183–211.

11. For discussions on the parting of ways of the Christianity from other Jewish sects see J. D. G. Dunn, *The Partings of the Ways* (London: SCM Press; Philadelphia: Trinity Press International, 1991); and J. Neusner, *Messiah in Context: Israel's History and Destiny in Formative Judaism* (Philadelphia: Fortress Press, 1984). See also W. S. Green, "Messiah in Judaism: Rethinking the Question," in *Judaisms and their Messiahs at the Turn of the Christian Era*, eds. J. Neusner, W. S. Green, and E. S. Freichs (Cambridge: Cambridge University Press, 1987), 1–13.

12. G. Scholem, "Toward Understanding the Messianic Idea in Judaism," in *The Messianic Idea in Judaism*, ed. G. Scholem (New York: Schocken Books, 1971), 1–36; see also Franz Mussner, *Tractate of the Jews: The Significance of Judaism for Christian Faith* (Philadelphia: Fortress Press, 1984), 80.

of his coming again at the end of times (Mark 13:26ff) as well as Jesus' messianic consciousness in a manner that necessitated that they "interiorise" God and "individuate" the Messiah – the Christ. The logic of Christ's conversion proclamation, his expiatory death, his prediction of his second coming which will culminate in annihilation of the antichrist and inauguration of a new heaven and a new earth, all seem to show that Jesus too was aware of his messianism.

The Christian canon depicts Christ the Messiah appealing to Isaiah for clarification of his authority to proclaim the reign of God. He also appeared to have understood what could as well be a mixture of Psalm 110:4 and Isaiah 53 as the background for his high priesthood. In his appeal to Isaiah and his sacrificial offering, we find compelling evidence for his messianic self-understanding. We see this messianic self-awareness particularly attested in at least three places: (1) in Matthew 11:5 (Luke 7:22) where in Jesus' reply to John the Baptist, he uses Isaiah 61:1–2 which was understood as the works of the Messiah. Then there are (2) Jesus' frequent usage of the curious self-reference "the son of man." A reading of "Son of Man" seen through the eyes of 1 Enoch gives a model of the "Anointed One" as an exalted heavenly figure with judicial functions. The New Testament sometimes appears to be using the wording of Daniel 7:13, 14 (Mark 13:21–22, 26, 14:62; Matt 25:31–46; Rev 1:7) which clearly envisages the Enochic reading. Then (3) the profound sense of self-awareness demonstrated on the cross by the statement – "it is finished." On the cross, Jesus referred simultaneously to his high priesthood as one who has offered a full atonement as well as to his exaltation to God's right hand (Psa 110:4; cf. Heb 1:3, 5:10, 7:26, 8:1, 9:24). The suggestion here is that he is not only the "dying one" but he is also the "risen one," "the exalted one" and "the anointed one" all rolled up in one figure – the Messiah (Isa 53; cf Mark 8:31, 9:31, 10:33–34; Phil 2:6–11).

## 1.3 Individuation of Wisdom

By the time of Christ, some modifications had happened in the Jews' use of Wisdom on account of a changed understanding of God's presence in their affairs. Now Wisdom was not just viewed as the gnomic limited to skills in practical affairs; it had evolved[13] to a cosmic principle that was understood to be the basis for purpose and order discernible in the universe (Joab 28:23, 25–27). Proverbs 8:21–31, ". . . wisdom is the cosmic thought, proceeding from God, creatively organizing and acting, and an objective reality even to God himself."[14]

At this point, Jewish literature begins to depict Wisdom not just as poetic personifications of wickedness and folly that we see in Proverbs 7:10ff or 9:13ff, but as a hypostasis. We see this in the Rabbinic literature of the time. In Sirach, we notice two occasions in which Wisdom is hypostasised: chapters 1 and 24. In chapter 24 verse 9, the writer presents a situation where Wisdom is explicitly said to be eternal and linked to the Trinity: "From eternity, in the beginning, he created me, and for eternity I shall not cease to exist." At Sirach 1:4, the origin of Wisdom is described in terms that are reminiscent of a similar case in Proverbs 8:22. As is the case with Proverbs 8, Sirach 24 presents observable parallels to Colossians 1:15. Here (Sir 24: 3a), the hypostasised Wisdom says she "came forth from the mouth of the Most High, the first-born before all creatures." This statement reflects the message of Colossians 1:15b where Christ the Word is said to be "first-born of all creation."

The other places where we see this hypostasisation is Sirach 24:19. In this text, Wisdom tells her listeners to "Come to me" in a manner very similar to Christ's invitation recorded in Matt 11:28. Like Jesus the Messiah was given the command to create (Enoch 30:8), Wisdom keeps souls from sin (Sir 24:22); indeed Wisdom has power to reward and punish (Prov 1:22ff, 3:16f, Amos 8:12, Isa 55:6). Wisdom toured the nations and found no place to dwell, so she returned to heaven to live with the angels. She is in heaven now (Enoch 41:1–3). These passages are intensified in Wisdom 7:25 which paints a fairly clear picture of how this hypostasis stands in relation to God:

> *For she is breath of the power of God,*
> *And a clear effluence of the glory of the Almighty;*

---

13. Walther Eichrodt advances the view that the change is as a result of Israel's contact with Hellenism. See Walther Eichrodt, *Theology of the Old Testament* (Philadelphia: The Westminster Press, 1967), 87.

14. Ibid., 85.

> *Therefore can nothing be defiled find entrance into her.*
> *For she is an effulgence from everlasting light,*
> *And an unspotted mirror of the working of God,*
> *And an image of his goodness.*

The above literature also indicates that Wisdom as a hypostasis has traces in creation and in other cultures. This situation provided an opportunity for dialogue between Israel's faith and the Hellenistic presentation. It is interesting however that on the one hand there is the admission of the availability of Wisdom far and wide, but by the same formula a line was drawn: Wisdom is everywhere, but it is to be found nowhere except in Israel. Nations have only heard rumors about her, ". . . God alone knows and possesses her" (Joab 28:27–28).

Yet in attempting to understand this hypostasis, separating Wisdom from either Logos or the Spirit has not always been easy. Indeed as Eichrodt says, the overlap has had a

> complicating effect which hampered clear exposition. In particular Wisdom and the Spirit, because of the similarity of their functions, easily combine to form a homogenous concept. Sometimes they are arranged in synonymous parallelism, as in Dan 5:11ff. or Wisd. 9:17; sometimes their functions merge, as in Philo and II (4) Esdras; sometimes they are identical, as in the Wisdom of Solomon, where Wisdom, like the Spirit is the breath of God, representing the divine power both in the physical and in the moral order. . . . Whereas in this document the Word is still clearly distinct from Wisdom, and appears as an independent angelic being, in Ben Sirach Wisdom is virtually born from the Word and in Philo is presented conversely as the mother of the Logos, with God as the Father. The Jewish teachers never found a method of organizing these various hypostases into a single system.[15]

---

15. Ibid., 90f.

## 1.4 The Preexistent Logos

The Jewish literature portrayed the Word as the cosmic power of the Creator God. This was understood as a declaration of God himself (Isa 40:26; 44:24; Pss 33:6, 9; 19:2ff; 104:7). The Word was hypostasized and shown to be having a role in creation (Col 1:15–20; Heb 1:4); and moreover John 1:1–18 referring to the Jewish exposition of Genesis 1:15 brings into the mix the pre-existent Word (Logos/*memra*). And so by the time John, Paul and the writer to the Hebrews are talking of a hypostasized Word, they are not introducing something new to the Jews of Jesus' time. In fact, they seem to be freely using the terms as they see them within the Jewish nomenclature and belief of the time. The usage of Logos/*memra* as a hypostasis was already available in the Jewish targums. The creation accounts in the targums indicate an interesting relationship between the hypostasized "Word (*memra*) of the Lord" and "God." In the *neofiti* targums, "the Word (*memra*) of the Lord" is a metonym for God. Thus for example in Genesis:

> *The word of the Lord* created the two large luminaries . . . (1:16) . . . the word of the Lord created the Son of man [i.e. man] . . . (1:27) . . . and *the Word of the Lord* said to them: "Be strong and multiply" (1:27) . . . And the seventh day *the Word of the Lord* completed the work which he had created . . . (2:2).[16]

What is so revealing is McNamara's comparison of Palestinian Targum Exodus 12:42 to John's prologue. The paraphrase of the text in *neofiti* and TJ 1 and 2 as identified by McNamara runs as follows: "The first night when the Lord was revealed above the earth to create it. The earth was void and empty and darkness was spread over the face of abyss. *And the Word [Memra] of the Lord was the light and it shone . . .*; and he called it the first night."[17] McNamara sees the rendering of the italicized part of the text as precisely what Apostle John says of the Logos: "In the beginning was the

---

16. Martin McNamara, *Targum and Testament: Aramaic Paraphrases of the Hebrew Bible – A Light on the New Testament* (Grand Rapids, MI: Eerdmans, 1972), 99. Note that some scholars reject the targamic *Memra* as a background to John's *Logos* as designation of Christ. Instead they see John influenced by the prophetic word (*dabar*) and word as it occurs in wisdom literature.

17. McNamara, *Targum and Testament*, 103.

Word . . . and the Word was God. In him was light and light shines in darkness" (John 1:1–3). McNamara's observation leads to the conclusion that the Apostle John no doubt obtained his hypostasized Logos (*Memra*) from what the "then current Jewish concepts of *Memra*, Glory and Shekinah (presence, dwelling) to express the incarnation and the mystery of Christ."[18]

Eichrodt sees a necessary connection between the Jewish hypostasized Word seen in the targums and the person of the Redeemer linked in two fundamental ways: (1) the Logos had to "reveal the divine will in a way which would confirm the personal and the spiritual nature of God's dealings with men . . . yet at the same time safeguard the hiddenness of the divine majesty"; and (2) the need for the Logos to comprehend both creation and redemption; "the valid permanent order and the new act of God, the static and the dynamic, the present and the future."[19] Thus, for Eichrodt, the New Testament Redeemer can only be understood in light of the Jewish hypostasis.

## 1.5 The Spirit of God

The Jewish tradition views this Spirit as generating from Yahweh and as belonging to Yahweh (Judg 13:25; Isa 32:15; 42:1; 59:21). In some cases the Old Testament goes as far as identifying the Spirit with Yahweh (Ps 139:7). According to Wainwright, the occurrence of Spirit in Psalm 139:7 is "equivalent to the Presence, which was a term used as a circumlocution for God."[20] In fact, other Old Testament texts separate the Spirit from God – although they closely link him with God as his power, and his breath that gives life, guides, and drives to action (see Ezek 37:9; Judg 3:10). The fact that the Old Testament identifies the Spirit with Yahweh, while at the same time suggesting that the two are indeed distinct entities, is a point worth noting.

Note that this marked independence of the Spirit, to the point that he is portrayed as a hypostasis – a separate entity – is part of the deepening of the working of the Spirit undertaken by the Jewish prophets. We see a

---

18. Ibid., 102–104; cf. Eichrodt, *Theology of the Old Testament*, 79.
19. Eichrodt, *Theology of the Old Testament*, 80.
20. A. W. Wainwright, *The Trinity in the New Testament* (London: SPCK, 1962), 30.

situation where the Holy Spirit is seen as a personal subject and applies the divine power within him to a particular effect. His work is broadened beyond the age of salvation; instead the Spirit is now depicted as the power which has maintained Israel's history (Isa 63:11ff.),[21] the "the nation's guide and protector in the present,"[22] the comforter and helper of individuals, and the one who brings "greater and greater areas of life within the scope of his dominion." Thus as Eichrodt explains, "political activity, and the whole field of art, whether it be inspired poetry or many varieties of craftsmanship, are subsumed under the operation of the spirit, and any skill in these directions are thankfully venerated as given by [him]."[23]

Whereas the Spirit is God's hypostasis that is the power behind the life of the people of God, he is also portrayed as "breath of life" – "the principle of life' (see Gen 2:7; Job 33:4). This "principle of life" must not dwindle away. Thus for Israel, power flowed from one God, who by virtue of his hypostasis *ruah* was the "principle of life" behind the existence the complex world around us. This operation of *ruah* of bringing about the diverse creation happened "without thereby depriving it of the diversity of its life or debasing it to the level of an inanimate machine."[24] Here then is a rejection of polytheism without sliding into deism and an acceptance of Yahweh as king, which resists the temptation to use the Sprit to explain the world along pantheistic and mystic lines.

Jewish thought also viewed *ruah* as God's instrument of the salvation history. They noticed the divine life-giving power in their nation's history: conquests, prophetic ecstasies, the healing of the sick, satisfying the hungry, recalling the dead to life. Indeed as Eichrodt says, the Jewish people saw and attributed it all to divine life-giving power:

> "At the mortal crises of the nation's history men hitherto completely unknown and unimportant, such as Gideon or Jephthah, could carry the dejected people with them to inspired military achievements; that the Nazarite Samson could

---

21. Other relevant passages include Ps 106:33; Zech 7:12; Isa 34:16; Hag 2:5.
22. Eichrodt, *Theology of the Old Testament*, 61.
23. Ibid., 62f. see also the following passages: Pss 51:11; 143:10; Prov 1:7; 9:10; 14:27; 15:33.
24. Eichrodt, *Theology of the Old Testament*, 48.

display the strength of a giant; that a diffident youth like Saul could compel the people to accept his leadership, and decisively defeat the insolent king of the Ammonites.[25]

There is also the view of *ruah* as the power of the divine in consummating the new age. Here, however, *ruah* is associated with the Holy God and man is depicted not only as totally incapable to live in the presence of God but also to do as God commands. In other words, mankind's relationship with God is no longer a private affair – it is given by the Spirit. As a consequence the prophets proclaimed divine transformation of men's hearts as the occasion for a paradigm shift: "emergence of a new cosmos out of the chaos of the present, made possible by such a divine intervention."[26] The focus here appears to be wider than the religious realm. It appears that the prophets here have in mind God's power for his people to live integrated and comprehensive lives. The divine life-giving power is not just for the agents; to the contrary, the divine power extends to and includes those who are led. They too must receive the power.[27]

## 1.6 Conclusion

The Jewish texts, canons and various interpretations seem to indicate both plurality and unity in the God of Israel. The Rabbinic thought of the time appears to have an idea of ητερος θεος.[28] This comes out clearly in the debate between Justin Martyr and Trypho.[29] Skarsaune summarizes what he sees as Justin's argument as follows: "Christ, not the Father, was the one who appeared in the theophanies of the Old Testament, and that he is to be identified with God's Wisdom, who is spoken of in the Bible as a second divine person, begotten by God, but not separated from him."[30] In

---

25. Ibid., 51.
26. Ibid., 58f.
27. For relevant scriptural references: Jer 31:31ff. talks of a situation that has arisen as a result of God's direct work. The same theme is carried in Isa 11:9. Other references discussing more or less the same theme are Zech 12:10; Joel 2:18ff.; 3:1f. The others are Isa 11:2; 42:1, cf. 61:1; 32:15; 44:3; Ezek 39:29; 11:19; 36:26f.
28. See Justin's *Dialogue with Trypho the Jew*, chapter 10–19, chapter 55–63.
29. *Dial.* 55.1.
30. O. Skarsaune, "Is Christianity Monotheistic? A Perspective on a Jewish/Christian Debate," *Studia Patristica* 29 (1957): 357; cf. *Dial.* 56–62, 126–129.

response to this thesis, Trypho does not say that that particular position destroys the Christian claim to monotheism, in fact, Trypho already believes that the Scripture may know a ητερος θεος.³¹ Instead, Trypho is portrayed as commending the Christians for retaining the fundamental part of the Torah; namely, the one against idolatry. The implication of this submission of the pre-Nicene sources is that the divinity of Christ and of the Holy Spirit does not reject the Jewish understanding of monotheism. In fact, there is a general lack of awareness in the Rabbinic thought that the admission of the divinity of the Son and of the Holy Spirit may create theological problems to the Jewish concept of monotheism.³² If such awareness were there, Justin would not have raised the issue of ητερος θεος with Trypho, for such a debate would have hurt Justin's case. Trypho, on the other hand, would have raised our attention to the incompatibility of the idea of ητερος θεος with the monotheism in his dialogue with Justin since the point of contention would be known to be untrue by everyone. Note also that before Justin, Philo in *Qu. Gen.* II.62 had already written about the *Logos* as δευτερος θεος and the Jewish thought of the time did not seem to have an issue to raise against such a position.

A third-century Rabbinic statement that is recorded in the *Babylonian Talmud, Megilla* 13a (Socino trans., 74) and attributed to Rabbi Johanan takes this argument further. The statement defines whoever rejects idolatry as a "Jew," that is "one who proclaims the unity (of God)." Skarsaune has noted a Hebrew wordplay here: "'*Jehudi*' is modified to '*Jechidi*,' one who proclaims that God is one, '*echad*.' So, the one who proclaims the unity or the one-ness of God is the one who rejects idolatry."³³ According to this criterion, as Skarsaune has noted, the Christians of the third-century qualified as *Jechidim*. In other words they qualified as worshipers of Yahweh of Israel under the same rubric of Jewish monotheism although they maintained an understood plurality in God.³⁴

---

31. Skarsaune, "Is Christianity Monotheistic?," 362.
32. Ibid., 355.
33. Ibid., 360, 361.
34. A more extensive parallel of this understanding of a "Jew" is available in *Esther Rabbah* 6:2, trans. H. Freedman and M. Simon, London, 1939, 73f. This understanding of a "Jew" that included the Christians continues until the start of the 7th century AD. This date coincides with the conclusion of the Babylonian Talmud and the rise of the Muslim

By the fourth century we notice that the questioning of the monotheistic stand of the Christian faith was not a Jewish-Christian problem, rather it was an inner-Christian problem. This is shown in the works of Tertullian, *Adversus Iudaeos*. In this book Tertullian uses Justin's *Dialogue* as one of his authorities. Justin had in this book raised the issue of the Trinity. Tertullian completely ignores the discussion in his argument against the Jews. Instead, he leaves the problem of ητερος θεος and whether the theology of this second divine person and the third divine person threatens biblical monotheism for his other book, *Against Praxeas*.[35] The significance of Tertullian's presentation in *Adversus Iudaeos* is that it helps us to see that the Trinity-Monotheism tension is not a Christian-Jewish problem, but that it is an inner-Christian problem.[36] The controversy began within Christianity itself and among people who held high offices within the communion of faith.[37] They are the ones who advanced what became known as the Monarchianism of the second and the third centuries and not Judaism.[38] Both Tertullian and Origen,[39] themselves firm proponents of separate υποςταςεις, are in fact on record as having named Christians and not Jews as their opponents[40]

---

empire (see L. Teugels, "The Background of the Anti-Christian Polemics in Aggadat Bereshit," *Journal of the Study of Judaism* XXX, no. 2 [1999]: 178–208, note 3).

35. Tertullian, *"Adversus Iudaeus"* (An Answer to the Jews, trans. S. Thelwal), in *Ante-Nicene Fathers: Translations of the Writings of the Fathers Down to AD 325*, vol. III, eds. A. Roberts and J. Donaldson (Grand Rapids, MI: Eerdmans, 1951). See also his other writing *"Against Praxeas"* and *"De Carne Christi,"* trans. D. Holmes, in *Ante-Nicene Fathers: Translations of the Writings of the Fathers Down to AD 325*, vol. III, eds. A. Roberts and J. Donaldson (Grand Rapids, MI: Eerdmans, 1951).

36. Skarsaune, "Is Christianity Monotheistic?," 359.

37. H. A. Wolfson, *The Philosophy of Church Fathers: Faith, Trinity and Incarnation* (Cambridge, MA: Harvard University Press, 1970), 577.

38. Ibid., 581–585.

39. Origen, "On the Gospel of John," in *Ante-Nicene Fathers: Translations of the Writings of the Fathers Down to AD 325*, vol. III, eds. A. Roberts and J. Donaldson (Grand Rapids, MI: Eerdmans, 1951).

40. Wolfson, *The Philosophy of Church Fathers*, 581. See also J. H. O. Kombo, *The Doctrine of God in African Christian Thought* (Leiden: Brill, 2007), 54–56.

CHAPTER 2

# Testimonies of the Early Church: Christian Identity, Theological Language and the Creeds

## 2.1 Introduction

Identity debates are known to generate great passions. In a generation characterized by so much competition and downturns, feasts and sobs, the voices particularly of the underclass and the downtrodden are most likely going to be raised in a stampede for the already burdened listenership. Christian talks are no exception to this, particularly given that the ever dominant Postmodernism and its trappings in one part of the world, and the call to cultural renaissance in the other, seem to place matters of religious significance in abeyance. To remain relevant, the temptation in Christian scholarship has been to move away from the homogenizing factor into participation in candid inquiries which seek to explain what it means to share in this or that gender, race, history, nationality, place, sexual orientation, religious beliefs and ethnicity.

There is no doubt that the Christian shares in social processes in which everyone participates in the context of changing historical conditions. Indeed, Christian scholarship ought to demonstrate leadership in such discourses. These pursuits, however, are not to replace genuine search into what constitutes the identity of the Christians and what the Christians must believe. The Christians, regardless of their geo-political, socio-cultural, gender or historical conditions, have a high level of homogeneity in God who calls us in Christ to a fellowship with him in the Holy Spirit.

This homogeneity, which the church Fathers discerned in the gospel, is our identity and it must not take back seat.

## 2.2 Christian Identity: The Third Race Question

The old Christian tradition's approach to the issue of identity is as incisive as it is inspiring. Early Christianity proceeded from the point of view that it was a community of strangers in the world. For them, Christ, who had so powerfully contextualized God, was their dwelling, so they did not see themselves as citizens of any particular country. The letter to Diognetus offers an impressive elaboration of this position:

> The Christians are distinguished from other men neither by country, nor by language, or the customs which they observe. For they neither inhabit cities of their own, nor employ a peculiar form of speech, nor lead a life which is marked out by any singularity. . . . Inhabiting Greek as well as barbarian cities, according as the lot of each of them has determined, and following the customs of the natives in respect to clothing, food, and the rest of their ordinary conduct, they display to us their wonderful and confessedly striking method of life. They dwell in their own countries, but simply as sojourners. As citizens, they share in all things with others, and yet endure all things as if foreigners. Every foreign land to them is their native country, and every land of their birth as a land of strangers.[1]

The position of the early Christians was that being in Christ exceeded all human identities. It didn't matter where the Christian lived, his or her nationality, or ethnicity, since in Christ there was neither Greek nor Jew, barbarians nor Scyth (Col 3:11). Everything belonged to Christ.[2]

---

1. *Ad Diognetum* 5. See the English translation at www.newadvent.org/fathers under the author "Mathetes."

2. Note that this tradition is founded on the preaching of the Apostles. Peter (1 Pet 2 and 4) and the author of Hebrews (11:13-16) speak of Christians as foreigners. But Paul (2 Cor 5:1) and John (18:36) also speak as much.

The Ante-Nicene and the Nicene fathers held firmly to this position. Consequently their belief in the truth that the personal coming of God to man in the Old Testament and the realization of the same in the incarnation of the Son and the outpouring of the Holy Spirit was, to say the least, a continuation of their identity discourse. Indeed as St Augustine was later to say, the Trinity talk was the starting point of this new identity as it was the beginning of the Christian faith – *initium fidei*. The early Christians seem not only to have given great prominence to how they wished to understand the glorious God they had come to know in Christ, but they also clearly saw the definition of the Trinity as indicative of their identity.

The streams of creeds that flowed in abundance by the fourth century, and were in regular use in the churches, were magisterial statements on the Trinity and therefore they were dogmatic statements, but they also functioned as statements of Christian identity. The word "creed" comes from the Latin word *credo*, meaning "I believe." Note that the emphasis here is belief in God and not in statements about God. The creeds thus expressed that the church believed in the Triune God over and against the alternatives that were available in the surrounding culture, but they also stated commitment into membership and therefore immersion into an emerging yet profoundly different community – the Christian community.

Justin, Tertullian, Athanasius, the Cappadocians, and Augustine were all aware that they were not Jews and that the way they wished to explain the God they worshiped differed significantly from the perspective the Jews held. They also knew that they were Greco-Romans, but they sought to break with that culture because the God they knew and worshiped was Yahweh and not *theos* as conceived in Gnosticism.

For some time, mainstream Christianity functioned as part of Judeo-Christianity. The movers of mainstream Christianity needed to bring this to an end. There are two distinct aspects of the concept of Judeo-Christianity worth highlighting. On the one hand, there is gamut of heresies that arose out of Judaism but claimed Christian identity, and on the other hand there are the cultural forms of Judeo-Christianity.[3] The cultural forms of Judeo-Christianity were really new systems of operation "with its own particular

---

3. B. J. F. Lonergan, *The Way to Nicea. Dialectical Development of Trinitarian Theology* (Philadelphia: Westminster Press, 1976), 18.

type of imagination, its own strange manner of conception and mode of speech."⁴ The heresies in a sense flowed from and were preceded by the cultural form of Judeo-Christianity, which did not only give them a soft landing but also provided them with the religious logic and nomenclature.

The cultural form of Judeo-Christianity was heavily tinged with the Gnostic and Neoplatonic influences. According to this scheme, God was seen not as Creator who loves his creation but as a God beyond being who was not only overly transcendent but who existed in multiple personalities. This system did not appreciate creation as a reflection of the work of God, instead it attributed the existence of the material world to the work of a lesser, evil deity. Consequently, according to this scheme of things, all that is material is unholy and ungodly. Some of the well-known heterodoxies that sprung from this cultural form are the Ebionites (Jesus is the greatest prophet but not the son of God), Elkasites (a simple prophet who had many reincarnations), Christian Zealotism (Jesus is an ordinary man; he had nothing to do with the creation of the world as that was done by angels), Samarito-Christian Gnosis, Sethians and Ophites as well as the Carpocrates (these groups agree on the conception that Jesus was just the son of Joseph and was not in any way different from other men).⁵

As mainstream Christianity steered clear of Judeo-Christianity in all its arrays, it got into a phase where it needed to deal with contradictions that existed within itself as it journeyed. In the third century AD, Paul of Samosata, Bishop of Antioch, taught that God, being One, could not appear substantially on earth; therefore he could not have become man in Jesus Christ, but rather filled the man, Jesus, with his Logos and power. Lucian of Antioch, his follower, believed that the Logos became man in Christ; however, Lucian's Logos was a lower, created essence and not fully God. Arius, one of Lucian's pupils, fully absorbed Lucian's Logos concept. In AD 311 Arius was ordained a presbyter in the church at Alexandria. Also in the third century AD, Sabellius had taught that the Father, Son

---

4. Ibid., 19.

5. J. Danielou, *The Theology of Jewish Christianity*, trans. and ed. J. A. Baker (London: Darton, Longman and Todd, 1964), 55–85. See also his *A History of the Christian Doctrine before the Council of Nicea*, vol. I, trans. and ed. J. A. Baker (London: Darton, Longman and Todd, 1964).

and the Holy Spirit are different modes or aspects of one God, rather than three distinct persons. Tertullian put a spirited fight against this teaching which he aptly labelled "Patripassianism," from the Latin words *patris* for "father," and *passus* "to suffer" because it implied that the Father suffered on the Cross[6] so that by AD 220, Sabellius faced excommunication as a heretic by Pope Calixtus. Elsewhere in Asia Minor and around AD 230, the same teaching also known as modalistic monarchianism was being pushed by Noetus, a presbyter of the church of Asia Minor. Noetus was ably counteracted by Hippolytus.[7]

In undertaking to understand the God they worshiped, the fathers looked to the New Testament writings for identity models. Once again these questions dominated their appropriation of the Scripture: Who were they? Who did they want to become? In the New Testament, they saw the triple identity in Peter: a race, a nation, a people (see 1 Pet 2:9). They found another triple identity in Paul: Jews, Greeks and community of faith (1 Cor 10:32). The logic was clear – they were who they were because of who their God was. Here then was the basis for developing a unique Christian consciousness distinct from that of the Greeks and that of the Jews. Kwame Bediako observes that by the "middle of the second century AD, the understanding of the Christian faith as 'the new . . . third way' had in fact become 'the Church's basal conception of history.'"[8] This identity, however, it must be noted, took shape in the context of finding how to talk about the mystery God whom they had come to know in Christ and worshiped in the Spirit.

## 2.3 Theological Language: Ousia, Hypostasis, Persona, Prosopon

If the Christian identity coalesced around how to talk about the God they had come to know in Christ and worshiped in the Spirit, there was also the

---

6. Tertullian in his work "*Adversus Praxeam*," Chapter II. Note that the Patripassianism in this context is used as an epithet against Praxeas, an early anti-Montanist, and not here applied to Sabellianism.

7. Kenneth S. Latourette, *A History of Christianity: Volume I: Beginnings to 1500* (New York: HarperCollins, 1975), 144–146.

8. K. Bediako, *Theology and Identity* (Oxford: Regnum Books, 1992), 38–39.

requirement for the theological language. How were they to speak about this gracious God? They had entered the Hellenistic world; as such they had to break from the Talmudic use of anthropomorphic language in putting forth the God they worshiped in Christ. Two reasons are worth advancing here for loss of favor with anthropomorphisms. The first reason was simply that anthropomorphisms were incapable of sufficiently conveying the utter difference and the complete otherness of "the Father of the universe" and "God unbegotten" to the changed audience. Continued use of anthropomorphisms in the Greco-Roman world would have the effect of ultimately undervaluing the significance of the Incarnation both in its substantive form and as a hermeneutic principle. The other reason appears to be theological. Anthropomorphisms, the Fathers believed, tended to image God and as such were seen to hinder free transmission of God's word. As far as the Fathers were concerned, all images used in speech and thought of God were to be used solely as transparent media through which the word of God was heard and under no circumstance should such a speech image God.[9]

The task then was to find words within the Greco-Roman conceptual framework which would express the unity (one God) and the differentiation (Father, Son and Holy Spirit) without undervaluing or giving pre-eminence to the one or to the other. The Fathers preferred the terms *ousia* and *hypostasis*. In theologic and philosophic contexts of the time, *ousia*, Lossky explains:

> The term *ousia* is frequently employed by Aristotle, who defines it as follows: "That is principally, primarily and properly called *ousia* which is stated of no subject and which is in no

---

9. A good example of a Nicene theologian who used this argumentation is Gregory Nazianzen (see "Orations," in *Nicene and post-Nicene Fathers of the Christian Church*, vol. IX, ed. P. Schaff [Grand Rapids, MI: Eerdmans, 1891], 28.12ff.; 29.2; 31.7; 33.17). It is important to note, however, that anthropomorphism in and of itself is not a problem in theology. It only becomes a problem when we begin to see God as inherently anthropomorphic and when our language about God is not controlled and adapted by whom God has revealed himself to be. Otherwise, since it is human beings who must know God, there is a level of anthropomorphism which is ineradicable, or else as Mackintosh once said: "What the conception of God may become when once the life-blood of anthropomorphism has been drained out, we see in the God of Mohammed. The Deity pictured in the Koran is 'like the desert, monotonous and barren, an unfigured surface, unresponsive immensity,'" (H. R. Mackintosh, *The Christian Apprehension of God*, 4th ed. [London: Student Christian Movement Press, 1934], 111).

subject – for example, this man, or this horse. We call "second ousias" (*deuterai ousiai*) those species wherein the "first ousias" exist with their corresponding description: thus, "this man" is specifically man and generically animal. Man and animal, then, are called "second ousias." In other words, "first ousias" are individual subsistences, the individual subsisting; "second ousias" essences, in the realistic sense of the word. *Hypostasis*, without having the value of a philosophical term, signifies in current terminology that which really subsists, subsistence (from the verb *hyphistamai*, to subsist).[10]

The Fathers, Basil in particular, confined *ousia* (being, essence) to the one Godhead and applied *hypostases* to the three: Father, Son and the Holy Spirit. Andrew Louth notes that they used various analogies to elucidate how they intended to use the terms. For instance:

> Cats share the nature of being a cat (*ousia*), but each individual cat is an instance of a cat (*hypostasis*). They also characterized hypostasis as "mode of existence" . . . in contrast to what it was to be, . . . the different modes of existence in the Godhead being identified with unbegottenness in the case of the Father, being begotten in the case of the Son, and proceeding in the case of the Holy Spirit, while all these *hypostaseis* shared the same being or *ousia*.[11]

Lossky is careful to note that the two terms are actually synonymous: "*ousia* meaning an individual substance, while being capable at the same time of denoting the essence common to many individuals; *hypostasis*, on the other hand, meaning existence in general, but capable also of application to individual substances."[12] But the West adopted another term *persona, prosopon* as equivalent to *hypostasis*. They did so because hypostasis had a tritheistic connotation in the West. But just as the West had their

---

10. Vladimir Lossky, *The Mystical Theology of the Eastern Church* (Crestwood, NY: St. Vladimir's Seminary Press, 1976), 50.

11. Andrew Louth, *St. John Damascene: Tradition and Originality in Byzantine Theology* (Oxford, England: Oxford University Press, 2004), 96.

12. Lossky, *The Mystical Theology*, 51.

misgivings, the East too worried that *persona* and *prosopon* had modalistic undertones. To solve the impasse, Basil the Great explained, as Louth notes "that the term *hoousion* does not mean that there is a divine *ousia* different from the divine person, or that there is some divine *ousia* underlying them."[13] *Ousia*, Basil insisted, is the Father's *ousia*, which he shares with the Son by begetting him and with the Holy Spirit by spiration. The technical theological usage of the terms therefore assigned the two synonyms different meanings to distinguish "that which is common – *ousia*, substance or essence – from that which is particular – *hypostasis* or person."[14] They acknowledged that the mystery of God remained, however the terms provided the media through which the Oneness of God and Threeness of Father, Son and Holy Spirit could be expressed. And so, says Lossky:

> Though the Latins might express the mystery of the Trinity by starting from one essence in order to arrive at the three persons; though the Greeks might prefer the concrete as their starting point (that is to say, the three hypostases), seeing in them the one nature; it was always the same dogma of the Trinity that was confessed by the whole of Christendom before the separation.[15]

## 2.4 The Creeds

The creeds were framed in the context of search for appropriate theological language for the idea of the Trinity as a subset of the bigger Christian identity question. In their correct historical settings, the creeds served to define and to railroad the basis for ecclesiastical fellowship. They strived to work out a vision for unity of the local as well as the universal church and a basis for witness to those outside the church. In doing this, they offered public standard for church discipline and a concise benchmark by which bishops and ministers were constantly evaluated. In this case they did not only function as depository and guardian of orthodox faith but they were

---

13. Louth, *St. John Damascene*, 97.
14. Lossky, *The Mystical Theology*, 51.
15. Ibid., 52.

also a useful tool for checking new teachings arising within the church. Samuel Miller has, by making reference to the Apostles Creed, illustrated these concerns rather extensively:

> In the fourth century, when the Church was still more agitated by the prevalence of heresy, there was a still louder demand for accredited tests, by which the heretics were to be tried and detected. Of this demand there never was a more striking instance than in the Council of Nicea, when the heresy of Arius was under the consideration of that far-famed assembly. When the Council entered on the examination of the subject, it was found extremely difficult to obtain from Arius any satisfactory explanation of his views. He was not only as ready, as the most orthodox divine present, to profess that he believed the Bible; but he also declared himself willing to adopt, as his own, all the language of the Scriptures, in detail, concerning the person and character of the blessed Redeemer. But when the members of the Council wished to ascertain in what sense he understood this language, he discovered a disposition to evade and equivocate, and actually, for a considerable time, baffled the attempts of the most ingenious of the orthodox to specify his errors, and to bring them to light. He declared that he was perfectly willing to employ the popular language on the subject in controversy; and wished to have it believed that he differed very little from the body of the Church.

Accordingly the evangelical faith went over the various titles of Christ plainly expressive of Divinity such as "God," "the true God," the "express image of God," etc., to every one of which Arius and his followers most readily subscribed, claiming a right, however, to put their own construction on the scriptural titles in question. After employing much time and ingenuity in vain, in endeavoring to drag this artful chief from his lurking places, and to obtain from him an explanation of his views, the Council found it would be impossible to accomplish their object as long as they permitted him to entrench himself behind a mere general profession of belief in the Bible.

They therefore did what common sense, as well as the word of God, had taught the Church to do in all preceding times, and what alone can enable her to detect the artful advocate of error. They expressed, in their own language, what they supposed to be the doctrine of Scripture concerning the Divinity of the Savior: in other words, they drew up a confession of faith on this subject, which they called upon Arius and his disciples to subscribe. This the heretics refused; and were thus virtually brought to the acknowledgment that they did not understand the Scriptures as the rest of the Council understood them, and, of course, that the charge against them was correct.[16]

The Council of Nicea (325) through the bishops in formulating the Apostles' Creed indicated in no uncertain terms their confession of Jesus Christ as fully divine, not created. On the basis of that they formulated the clause "God of God, light of light, true God of true God, begotten, not made, of one substance with the Father." The last portion of the Apostles' Creed was particularly significant in the *homoousios* debate. Here *homoousios,* which literally means of the same substance, same essence, or one being, is used to convey the position that what God is in his essence, the Son of God is also.

The Council of Nicea (325) did not focus their discussion on the Holy Spirit. Instead it merely said, "we believe in the Holy Spirit," and did not get into the what and the who of this hypostasis. This would not be a matter of concern for the church until the Council of Constantinople. Arius' position was that the Holy Spirit was a created spirit being; the bishops on the other hand confessed that the Holy Spirit is divine in the same way as the Son. The Council of Constantinople (AD 381) affirmed that Jesus is fully divine, eternal, not created. They also affirmed the equal divinity of the Holy Spirit. They taught that the Father is God, the Son is God, and the Holy Spirit is God, yet there is only one God – one God in three *Persona*. They did not explain how this is so – they just said that it *is* so. They felt compelled by Scripture to come to this conclusion. The result

---

16. Miller, "Utility and Importance of Creeds and Confessions," 21–22.

of this council is the creed which has come to be known as the Niceno-Constantinopolitan Creed, more commonly known by the shorter and more pronounceable name Nicene Creed. The creed is based on the creed of Nicea, reportedly edited at the council of Constantinople, but first seen in its final form seventy years later.

The Athanasian Creed or the *Quincunque Vult* (Latin for "whosoever wishes") has been in use since the sixth century AD. The creed focuses itself on the equality of the three hypostases of the Trinity. Divine majesty and characteristics are ascribed to the Father, the Son and the Holy Spirit each individually. The three are individually divine, yet they are not three gods, but one God. The creed further distinguishes the three hypostases from each other. It stated that the Father is neither made nor begotten; the Son is not made but is begotten from the Father; the Holy Spirit is neither made nor begotten but proceeds from the Father and the Son (*filioque*). The creed's teaching on Christ is more detailed than in the other two creeds and reflects familiarity with the conclusions of the Council of Ephesus (AD 431) and the definition of the Council of Chalcedon (AD 451). Among the major teachings the creed excludes are Sabellianism, Arianism, Nestorianism and Eutychianism.

## 2.5 Conclusion

Identity, theological language and the creeds worked concurrently and together in forming what Christianity had always known to be its doctrine of God. This doctrine in its various parts will for many years be the convergent point for many controversies and the symbol of belonging in the orthodox faith. Indeed, as Samuel Miller says in the context of creeds and confessions, it is only from those

> . . . who have either far departed or at least begun to depart, from "the faith once delivered to the saints," almost exclusively, do we hear of the "oppression," and the "mischief" of creeds and confessions. And is it any marvel that those who maintain the innocence of error should be unwilling to raise fences for keeping it out of the Church? Is it any marvel that the Arian, the Socinian, the Pelagian, and such as are verging

toward those fatal errors, should exceedingly dislike all the evangelical formularies which tend to make visible the line of distinction between the friends and the enemies of the redeemer? No; "men," as has been often well observed, "men are seldom opposed to creeds, until creeds have become opposed to them." . . .

We shall find, with few exceptions, that whenever a group of men began to slide, with respect to orthodoxy, they generally attempted to break, *if* not to conceal, their fall, by declaiming against creeds and confessions.[17]

Whereas Miller's concern in the excerpt above is for global Christianity, I find his contribution particularly significant to Christianity in the new heartlands. In the context of Africa, for instance, the Bible is perhaps the only library that most people have. It would be naive to think that since most people confess that they believe the Bible that they have actually remained true to the narrow path. Most heterodoxies say they believe the Bible. It appears that the actual nexus for any meaningful discourse on the doctrine of the Trinity, as indeed any other doctrine, is when we state in our own terms what we believe the Bible teaches. This way we will be able to separate genuine attempts to relate the Trinity to the African cultural consciousness from messianic forms and spiritists who, sensing much openness to Christianity in these regions, prey on weak souls to launch lives of their own.

---

17. Ibid., 25.

CHAPTER 3

# God as Essence

## 3.1 Platonism, Neo-Platonism, Aristotelianism and Theology

Paul Ricoeur's great contribution to the scholarship on Plato and Aristotle in which he sees these two philosophers as having laid the ontological foundations of what has become the Western philosophy is most invaluable to this present work. As part of the process of reaching this conclusion, Ricoeur explores a debate between Plato and Aristotle about being, essence, and substance and ultimately depicts Plato as a philosopher of essence and Aristotle a philosopher of substance. Engaging with Paul Ricoeur allows one to very quickly see two major philosophers (Plato and Aristotle), who address themselves to three fundamental issues (being, essence, and substance),[1] and how this will be important for this nuance of theology.

This present chapter not only attempts to link three key theologians (St Augustine, Boethius, and Aquinas) and their theological formulations of the Trinity to Plato's and Aristotle's concepts of being, essence and substance, but it also argues that "God as Essence" has over the years evolved to become a formidable and an independent model of presenting the doctrine of the Trinity. Care is taken to note that focus of this study shall be trained on Neoplatonism which refers to a school of philosophy that took shape in the third century AD, based on the teachings of Plato and the Platonists. The philosophy is often credited to Plotinus (c. AD 205–270)

---

1. Paul Ricoeur, *Being, Essence and Substance in Plato and Aristotle*, trans. David Pellauer and John Starkey (Cambridge: Polity, 2013).

and his disciple Porphyry (AD 232–c.300) who is credited with expanding and assembling the ideas into the six Enneads. After the fall of the Roman Empire (AD 476), the works of the Peripatetic school were lost to the West, but in the East they were incorporated into early Islamic philosophy which would play a large part in the revival of Aristotle's doctrines in Europe and the Middle East.

## 3.2 St Augustine: God as the Godhead

Augustine follows Neoplatonic logic in his formulation of the doctrine of the Trinity. Throughout his discourse of the Trinity, there appears a clear connection between the Neoplatonic doctrine of the "One" and his favorite choice of the abstract concept of the "Godhead." Thus for him, God meant the Godhead or essence.[2] He discusses Godhead as the highest principle; more or less the same way as Neoplatonism presents the idea of the "One." Godhead is therefore entirely undifferentiated. In other words, Godhead is completely simple and without multiplicity. Here then Augustine discovers one of the three types of substances in Neoplatonism: the one that is eternally stationary. Augustine sees in this category not many substances but one substance who in itself is immovable and imperishable; it acts without the intervention of any other being while it is at the same time the source and origin of all. Everything that is proceeds from it; it is the most perfect intelligence – God

For Augustine, the mind of God contains the eternal, changeless Ideas, Forms, or Archetypes of all things in a manner similar to what we see in Plato's idea of "form." These creative Ideas are independent of matter. They are the *rationes seminales* which the divine Creative Will developed within time into seen forms. The view that these Ideas are in the Word goes back to Philo and the Stoic *Logoi Spermatikoi*, and from Augustine they would be passed into medieval theology. To Augustine, created things tend toward

---

2. Augustine, "*De Trinitate*," in *Basic Writings of St Augustine*, vol. II, ed. E. J. Oates (New York: Random House, 1948), 1:8:15.

non-being; but so long as they exist, they must assume some form. That form is the reflection of the eternal and immutable Form.³

Augustine's discussion of the Son and the Holy Spirit is very similar to what we see of Plotinus' doctrine of emanation. By this doctrine Plotinus indicated a relationship between the One, Intelligence and the Soul. For him, Intelligence emanates from the One and the Soul emanates from Intelligence. In this process the emanating entity does not diminish, rather, it remains outside its product while at the same time it is present within it. Compare this to Augustine's link between the Father, Word and Wisdom:

> If this is said of the Son (for some will have it understood that the Son Himself spoke either by the prophets or in the prophets), whither was He sent except to the place where He already was? For He who says, "I fill heaven and earth," was everywhere. But if it is said of the Father, where could He be without His own word and without His own wisdom, which "reacheth from one end to another mightily, and sweetly ordereth all things?" But He cannot be anywhere without His own Spirit. Therefore, if God is everywhere, His Spirit also is everywhere. Therefore, the Holy Spirit, too, was sent thither, where He already was. For he, too, who finds no place to which he might go from the presence of God, and who says, "If I ascend up into heaven, Thou art there; if I shall go down into hell, behold, Thou art there;" wishing it to be understood that God is present everywhere, named in the previous verse His Spirit; for He says, "Whither shall I go from Thy Spirit? or whither shall I flee from Thy presence?" (Ps 139:7)⁴

For Plotinus the emanation is completely involuntary. It is a result of an inner necessity – what is full must overflow, what is mature must beget. Note that in the logic of Augustine, what is common to the hypostases is the "One." The Father is a hypostasisation of the "One." The Father is personally concrete and distinguished from the Son. He is the hypostasis

---

3. R. H. Nash, *The Light of the Mind: St. Augustine's Theory of Knowledge* (Lexington, KY: The University Press of Kentucky, 1969), 6.

4. Augustine Bishop of Hippo, "Confessions Book 2," in *Nicene and Post Nicene Fathers of the Christian Church*, vol. I, ed. P. Schaff (Grand Rapids: Eerdmans, 1994), ch 5:7.

which causes the person of the Son by the act of eternal generation. The Father is also the cause of the Holy Spirit by the act of eternal procession. Again the relationship between the Father and the Son and the Holy Spirit is shown by Augustine to be involuntary and spontaneous.

Consequently, Augustine was able to concretize the hypostases and to distinguish the same from each other only by their relations with each other. Augustine saw two types of relations (Father-Son and Spirator-Spirit) that distinguish Father and Son from each other and Father and Spirit from each other. In Augustine's consideration, the problem was how the Holy Spirit was to be distinguished from the Son. In answer to this problem, Augustine explained that the Holy Spirit is caused by the Father as well as by the Son.[5]

---

**Major Features of Neoplatonism**

1) The visible, tangible forms of the physical world are based on immaterial models, called Forms or Ideas.
2) Tangible forms are transitory, unstable, and imperfect, whereas ideal Forms are eternal, perfect, and unchanging.
3) Physical forms are many and diverse, but ideal Forms are single and unified.
4) There is a definite hierarchy of value on these qualities:
    a) Eternity is superior to the temporal;
    b) Unity is superior to division;
    c) The immaterial is superior to the material.
5) The fleeting physical world that humankind inhabits becomes a kind of flawed manifestation of a perfect and eternal model that can be perceived only by the intellect, not by the senses.

---

5. Augustine, "*De Trinitate,*" 5:6, 8, 14, 15. Augustine from these texts seems to suggest that to call these subsistent relations 'person' is a mere linguistic usage. In his own words we can speak of persons "so that we not be altogether silent when asked what three, while we confess that they are three" (Augustine, "*De Trinitate,*" 5:10).

6) The "One" is a transcendent, ineffable, divine power, the source of everything that exists. It is complete and self-sufficient. Its perfect power overflows spontaneously into a second aspect, the Intelligence (Mind or Nous), which contemplates the power of the "One." By contemplating the "One," the Intelligence produces Ideas or Forms. The unity of the "One" thus overflows into division and multiplicity. These Forms are translated into the physical world through the creative activity of the World Soul. In the immaterial realm, the higher part of the Soul contemplates the Intelligence, while in the material realm, the lower part of the Soul acts to create and govern physical forms. The following are clear from this position:
   a) the existence of an ineffable and transcendent One;
   b) from the One emanated the rest of the universe as a sequence of lesser beings;
   c) Later Neoplatonic philosophers, added hundreds of intermediate gods, angels and demons, and other beings as emanations between the One and humanity;

The Soul, in descending from the immaterial to the material world, forgets some of its divine nature. All human individual souls, therefore, share in the divinity of the One and will eventually return to the divine realm from which they came, after they shed their physical bodies. Porphyry further developed Plotinus' ideas about the soul, asserting that individual human souls are actually separate from and lower than the World Soul. However, by the exercise of virtue and contemplation of the spiritual, the human soul can ascend from the lower, material realm, toward the highest good, the absolute beauty and perfection of the immaterial One.

## 3.3 Boethius: God as the Divine Substance

Medieval theology through Boethius modified the Augustinian usage of essence and updated it with Aristotle. His significance lies in the bridge his works builds between those of Augustine and Aquinas. He reinterprets the essence of God within the infrastructure of the concept of "form" as it occurs in Aristotle. He however uses "form" in a manner which signifies as "universal." This allows him to struggle with how the particular "universal" in question stands in relationship to the "concrete individual thing."[6]

For Boethius, God is his "essence" and that "essence" is the "form" that he has achieved – the divine substance. This divine substance or divine nature, explains Boethius, is "form without matter, and is therefore One, and its own essence."[7] God in this case therefore is what is universal to the three *personae*. God is a "pure form," or his "own essence." Elsewhere he says that "when we say God, we . . . denote a substance; a substance that is supersubstantial."[8] The three persons in the Boethian theology are only individual, concrete expressions of the universal (the essence or substance) with the same attributes as what is universal.

In fact, in Boethius the divine attributes are applied to the "Godhead." His argument is that the divine substance lies in the Godhead. In other words, God is simple and undifferentiated. He and his Substance (or essence) are one and the same. He is his own essence and the divine essence cannot be "distinguished either by accidents or by substantial differences belonging to a substrate"[9] The concept of "person" is traced to the idea of "mask." He writes that the word "person seems to be borrowed from a different source, namely from the masks which in comedies and tragedies used to signify different subjects of representation."[10] The Greeks called

---

6. G. B. Kerferd, "Aristotle," in *The Encyclopedia of Philosophy*, ed. P. Edwards (London: Collier Macmillan Ltd, 1967), 159; cf. A. M. S. Boethius, *The Theological Tractates and the Consolation of Philosophy*, rev. and trans. H. F. Stewart and E. K. Rand (London: William Heinemann, 1918), see section 5, 7.

7. Boethius, *The Theological Tractates*, 11.

8. Ibid., 17, 35.

9. Ibid., 13.

10. Ibid., 86f.

these "persons" or "masks" *prosopa* and the Latins called them *personae*.[11] As far as Boethius is concerned, he sees a substance with intelligence behind the mask.

> **Major Features of Aristotelianism**
> 1) Plato used the theory of Forms to explain reality but Aristotle preferred to start from the facts given by experience. Philosophy to him meant science whose aim was the recognition of the "why" in all things.
> 2) All change or motion takes place in regard to substance, quality, quantity and place.
> 3) There are three kinds of substances :
>    a) those alternately in motion and at rest, as the animals;
>    b) those perpetually in motion, as the sky;
>    c) those eternally stationary. The substances in this category are in themselves immovable and imperishable; indeed they are the source and origin of all motion.
> 4) Among these three types of substances, there must be one first being, unchangeable, which acts without the intervention of any other being. All that is, proceeds from it; it is the most perfect intelligence – God
>    a) The immediate action of this prime mover – happy in the contemplation of itself – extends only to the heavens;
>    b) The other inferior spheres are moved by other incorporeal and eternal substances, which the popular belief adores as gods.
>       i. The heavens are of a more perfect and divine nature than other bodies.
>       ii. In the center of the universe is the earth, round and stationary.
>       iii. The stars, like the sky, beings of a higher nature, but of grosser matter, move by the impulse of the *prime mover*.

---

11. Ibid., 87; see also Aquinas, *Summa Theologica*, I, q 29, art. 3. This is part of T. Aquinas, *Summa Theologica*, 3 Volumes, trans. Fathers of English Dominican Province (New York: Benzinger Brothers, inc., 1947).

> 5) For Aristotle, matter is the basis of all that exists; it comprises the potentiality of everything, but of itself is not actually anything. A determinate thing only comes into being when the *potentiality* in matter is converted into actuality. This is achieved by *form*, the idea existent not as one outside the many, but as one in the many, the completion of the potentiality latent in the matter. This concept will be very key in interpreting both Boethius and Aquinas.

## 3.4 The Influence of Islam and Judaism: God as His Non-Divisible Essence

The Early Islamic philosophy had more influence on the Christians' idea of God than theology has been prepared to accept. The Early Islamic philosophy is a period of intense philosophical development beginning in the second century AH (early 9th AD) and lasting until the sixth century AH (late 12th AD). The period began with al-Kindi in the ninth century and ended with Averros (Ibn Rushd) at the end of twelfth century. Thomas Aquinas appears to have been familiar with Mutazilite work and particularly Avicennism and Avorroism. The *Kalam*[12] appeared at the very beginning of this age.

The *Kalam* theology resuscitated the Jewish-Christian debates on the problem of monotheism. This time both Judaism and Islam joined hands and defined "one-ness or unity of God as having to do with his non-material and therefore non-composite and non-divisible essence."[13] In other words, the one-ness of God was understood to be the common substance and the three hypostases reduced to mere essential attributes.

The Christian-Muslim debates that dated from the early ninth century indicate that the Oriental-Christian apologists tried to explain to

---

12. *Kalam* is a rationalistic, philosophical theology that was developed by Moslem theologians in the ninth century that applied the categories of Aristotle to the Arabic thought. A standard monograph on this is H. A. Wolfson, *The Philosophy of the Kalam* (Cambridge, MA: Harvard University Press, 1976).

13. Skarsaune, "Is Christianity Monotheistic?," 348.

the Muslims the concept of the Triune God using the attributes ascribed to Allah in the Qu'ran.[14] The early approach identified the being of God with the Father. Then the Son and the Spirit merely became his attributes. This approach is seen in the Al Kindi's, *Apology*, which introduces wisdom and knowledge (alternatively life and knowledge) as the two essential attributes that together with the divine substance make a Trinity.[15] There are also instances where the Father is associated with one divine attribute. For example, by 1150–1200 two Muslim works (*Trinitizing the Unity* and *The Book of the Existing World*) explain that the Oriental-Arabic Christians taught that God's essence has the three attributes of Power (the Father), Knowledge (the Son), and Will (the Holy Spirit)[16]

The response of the Muslims and the Jews to this type of polemics is interesting. The Kalamic School of the Mutazilites,[17] for example, denied the existence of attributes in God altogether.[18] However, the dominant Muslim group in the school of Asharism[19] and the Jews accepted the existence of the attributes, but did not see how any of the attributes could ever exist as Trinitarian *personae*. Later in the high and late Middle Ages the Christian authors in the Latin West would adopt many of the arguments earlier posited by the Oriental-Arabic-Christian polemicists, who saw the one-ness of God as a common substance with three essential attributes that (by

---

14. H. A. Wolfson, "The Muslim Attributes and the Christian Trinity," *The Harvard Theological Review* 49 (1956): 1–18.

15. N. A. Newman, ed., *The Early Christian Muslim Dialogue: A Collection of Documents from the First Three Islamic Centuries (632-900)* (Hatfield, PA: Interdisciplinary Biblical Research Institute, 1993), 419–420.

16. Skarsaune, "Is Christianity Monotheistic?," 343.

17. Mutazilites derive from the Arabic *Mutazilah*, the first Islamic, systematic, theological school that was of tremendous influence in the Islamic world for many centuries. The Mutazilites saw their call as preserving the divine unity. However in pursuing this task, it chose, as Nasr explains, "a rationalistic interpretation of the Divinity which tended to view God more as a philosophical abstraction than as a reality who is the fountainhead of the revealed religion" (S. H. Nasr, "Islamic Conception of Intellectual Life," in *Dictionary of History of Ideas II (638-652)*, ed. P. P. Wierner [New York: Charles Scribner's Sons, 1973], 641). Mutazilism was challenged at the end of the ninth century by Asharism, an alternative systematic theological school which "opposed the rationalistic tendencies of the Mutazilites, sought to re-establish the concrete presence of God by charting a middle course between 'tashbih' and 'tanzih' or by giving anthropomorphic qualities to God on the one hand, and abstracting all qualities from him on the other hand" (Ibid., 642).

18. Wolfson, *The Philosophy of the Kalam*, 18–19, 132–143.

19. Nasr, "Islamic Conception of Intellectual Life," 642.

necessity) belong to the substance and are one with it.[20] Some of the early Latin-Western-Christian thinkers who used the Oriental-Arabic-Christian polemicists' style of constructing the doctrine of the Trinity and employed the substance-attributes model are William of Conches (d. 1145) and Peter Abelard (1079–1142). In these thinkers we see the triad Father = *potentia*, Son = *sapentia*, and Spirit = *voluntas* (in the case of William) and *benignitas* (in Abelard). The same triad occurs in Hugh of St Victor (1096–1141), except that this time more flexibility is accorded to the Holy Spirit: *bonitas sive benignitas, amor, voluntas*.[21] A similar trend is noticeable in the works of Anselm.

## 3.5 Thomas Aquinas: God as His Essence

The understanding of Thomas Aquinas' interpretation of the Latin West's doctrine of God cannot be abstracted from the philosophical and theological developments that were taking place in the high Middle Ages (11th to 13th centuries). It is on record that Aquinas' understanding of Aristotle is not inferior to that of Averros or Maimonides' – the great Muslim and Jewish Aristotelians.[22] There was also an ongoing interaction between the three monotheistic faiths: Christianity, Judaism and Islam. Aquinas would explain his unique faith (Catholic faith) not only in the light of his Aristotelian frame of thought but also in a context which had the powerful presence of the three faiths – Judaism, Christianity and Islam.

Aquinas begins his investigation into the nature of God by radically modifying the Aristotelian conception of simplicity of substance. In the sixth chapter of his *On Being and Essence*, Aquinas separates substance into three distinct categories: divine, spiritual, and material.[23] Aquinas sees the

---

20. D. J. Lasker, *Jewish Philosophical Polemics Against Christianity in the Middle Ages* (New York: Ktav Pub House, 1977), 13–20.

21. Ibid., 63, 64, 68, 207, n.177.

22. R. J. Henle, *St Thomas and Platonism: A Study of the Plato and Platonici Texts in the Writings of St. Thomas* (The Hague: Martinus Nijhoff, 1956), 7.

23. This division allows Aquinas to deal with the theological problem that occurs because of the existence of spiritual beings such as angels, which he includes in his second category, and the reality of the nature of man seen against the background of the spiritual reality in opposition to the nature of man and the rest of the created world. For Aquinas, man is a special case because he has a soul, but at the same time he has an animal body. Whereas Aristotle viewed man in a naturalistic way (Aristotle assumes that all substances

spiritual and the material categories as finite beings that have some aspects in common and fall within the same logical genus as both created spirits and bodies. The divine substance, however, is of an entirely different nature from that of bodies and of created spirits. There is only one divine substance; the identity of which is God.[24] By saying that the identity of the divine substance is God, Aquinas is appealing to the Aristotelian doctrine of the simplicity of substances: no substance consists of substances, or to put it in another way, "the substance of a thing is that which is peculiar to it."[25] In this particular case the divine substance is peculiar to God. God is his own form. The immaterial divine substance is organized in a manner that does not connote any relationship to anything in any way other than to God.

Having dealt with the problem of substance, matter and form, Aquinas now turns his attention to the issue of "essence." What is the essential property of the divine substance? In other words: Why is *this* substance God? The divine substance is God because the essence of God is present in the substance; it is the essence of a *prime mover*.[26] In other words, God is a necessary being whose very nature it is to exist. His existence cannot depend on anything external; rather, it is necessary as that is his nature. Existence is he and he is existence. In other words, it is not the case that God could have failed to have existence; his existence is his essence. God is "He Who Is" (*Qui est*), and "He Who Is" is the most proper name for God.[27]

Although essence and existence are identical in God, Aquinas believes the human mind cannot comprehend this identity because the divine essence cannot be known as it is in itself. In the thought of Aquinas, man

---

are material) and, therefore, put man in the same plane as animals, Aquinas saw man as possessing a soul united with the animal body. According to Aquinas, the human soul, being a spiritual substance, is capable of disembodied existence. See Aquinas, *Summa Theologica*, 1a, trans. Fathers of English Dominican Province (New York: Benzinger Brothers, inc., 1947), xxix, 3–4. Cf. Aristotle, *De Anima* (New York: Arno Press, 1976).

24. T. Aquinas, *On Being and Essence*, trans. and annotated J. J. O'Meara (New York: Newman, 1961), ch. 6.

25. Aristotle, *Metaphysics* (London: Dent, 1956), 1038b 9(1)(a).

26. Aristotle, *Metaphysics,* 1041a 4.

27. Aquinas, *Summa Theologica*, I, 13, II; cf. Aquinas, *Summa Contra Gentiles*, trans. A. C. Pegis, J. F. Anderson, and V. F. Bourke (Notre Dame, IN: University of Notre Dame Press, 1975), see sections I ch. 22 (First published in 1956 as *On the Truth of the Catholic Faith*).

cannot comprehend the divine essence because God is an immaterial being of an entirely different nature. However, we can comprehend the statement, "God exists."[28] We arrive at the knowledge that he exists, not through his essence, but through his effects.[29]

The final explanation of the relationship of essence and existence is found in Aquinas' cosmological proofs of God. The first starts from movement in the world and arrives at a concept of the *primum movens* [first cause of movement].[30] The second proceeds from effects in the world and arrives at the concept of the *causa prima* [first cause of change].[31] The third starts from the potential being of all things and arrives at the concept of the *ens per se necessarium* [something which must be].[32] The fourth begins with the gradation of beings in the world and arrives at the concept of the *maxime ens* [something which causes in all other things their being].[33] Finally, the fifth starts from the order of the world and arrives at the concept of someone with the highest *intellectus*.[34] To these five definitions Aquinas adds in each case: "*et hoc dicimus Deum*' – [and this we call God].

These proofs allowed Aquinas to understand the divine nature as the moving, causing, necessary, pure and intelligent Being. To God – who is thus named – can be predicated such attributes as almighty, omnipresent, omniscient, unchanging, infinite, and incomprehensible. As Berkhof has observed, these "omni-, un-, and in-, words" have dominated the doctrine of God for centuries because they gave expression to both the exaltedness and the firmness that people sought to find in God.[35]

After Aquinas discussed the existence and attributes of God under the rubric of what has become known in theological circles as *De Deo Uno*, the Godhead as the nature common to the three persons,[36] he turns to the

---

28. Aquinas, *Summa Theologiae*, I, 86–88; Aquinas, *Summa Contra Gentiles*, I ch. 3.
29. Aquinas, *Summa Theologiae*, I ch 11; cf. I *Distinctio* 3 q 1:a.2.
30. Aquinas, *Summa Theologica*, I, q. 2, a. 3.
31. Ibid.
32. Ibid.
33. Ibid.
34. Ibid.
35. H. Berkhof, *Introduction to the Study of Dogmatics*, trans. J. Vriend (Grand Rapids, MI: Wm B Eerdmans, 1985), 93.
36. Aquinas, *Summa Theologica*, I, qs. 1–26.

Trinity – *De Deo Trino*.[37] This approach, which separates the immanent Trinity from the economic Trinity, has in a way been considered the universal standard. Rahner argues "one cannot however appeal to tradition for the now standard division and order of the two treatises. It only came into general use since the *Sententia* of Peter Lombard were replaced by the *Summa* of St Thomas."[38]

Aquinas says, "As the Godhead is God, so the divine paternity is God the Father, who is a divine person."[39] What is interesting, however, is Aquinas' understanding of "divine Person." For him, the divine person signifies a relationship that subsists in the divine essence, "person means relation."[40] This is clearly a standard Augustinian position. In Aquinas' consideration, a divine person is actually an internal relation within the simple divine essence, the Godhead.

The Father *is* the "principle" not *from* a "principle." Clearly, Aquinas uses the concept principle to signify "that whence another proceeds,"[41] thus paternity.[42] The Son as Word. The Son alone is called the Word of God;[43] he proceeds from God and this procession is called generation.[44] "Word implies relation to creatures. For God, by knowing Himself knows every creature . . . because God by one act understands Himself and all things, His one only Word is expressive not only of the Father, but of all creatures."[45] The Holy Spirit is the procession of "love in God."[46] This position is similar to what Augustine had taught. In the words of Augustine, "Scripture teaches us that he is the Spirit neither of the Father alone, nor of the Son alone, but of both; and so his being suggests to us that mutual love

---

37. Ibid., qs. 27–43.
38. K. Rahner, *Theological Investigations* IV, trans. K. Smyth (London: Darton, Longman and Todd, 1966), 83.
39. Aquinas, *Summa Theologiae* I, q. 29, art. 4.
40. Aquinas, *Summa Theologica* I, q. 29, art. 4.
41. Ibid., q. 33, art. 1 & 4.
42. Ibid., q. 33, art. 2.
43. Ibid., q. 34, art. 2.
44. Ibid., q. 27, art. 2.
45. Ibid., q. 34, art. 3.
46. Ibid., q. 27, art. 4.

by which Father and Son love each other."[47] The way this procession of love is distinguished from the "other procession" is what Aquinas calls "relations of opposition." This appears from the fact that the Father has two relations; by one of these he is related to the Son, by the other to the Holy Spirit. But these two relations (generation and spiration) are not relations of opposition (to each other), and therefore they do not make two persons, but belong only to the one person of the Father. He explains himself as follows:

> The Son and the Holy Spirit must be related to each other by relations of opposition. Now there cannot be in God any relations opposed to each other, except relations of origin.... And opposite relations of origin are to be understood as of a *principle*, and of what is *from the principle*. Therefore it is necessary to say that either the Son is from the Holy Ghost; which no one says; or that the Holy Spirit is from the Son, as we confess.[48]

Aquinas' image of God is the dominant position within modern Catholicism. Mainline Protestantism also identifies with Aquinas' way of understanding God, as is clearly evident in the Belgic Confession. As Berkhof has noted, the Belgic Confession Article I "offers a definition of God by means of abstract omni- and in- words, and it is only from Article 17 onward that the love of Christ comes to be central – without however allowing this confession to modify the definition of God given in Article I."[49] This situation results from viewing God more in the context of *quid sit* – as a "being" – and, obviously, as contemplated within an abstract framework rather than from seeing him as he is revealed in Scripture.

## 3.6 Conclusion

We can say without fear of contradiction that the "God as essence" model of the Trinity is a hammer that has won many anvil. Its affinity to Neoplatonism and Aristotelianism as well as identity with St Augustine,

---

47. Augustine, *De Trinitate*, 15:17:27; cf. 6:5:7.
48. Aquinas, Summa Theologiae, I q. 36, art. 2.
49. Berkhof, *Introduction to the Study of Dogmatics*, 94.

Boethius and Aquinas indicate the range of influence and geographical spread as well as historical roots. For this interpretive model, Neoplatonism and Aristotelianism was an appropriate intellectual system of articulating God as they had known him in Christ. Indeed St Augustine and Boethius indicated to their contemporaries that the Aristotelian ontology was the appropriate medium of articulating reality. Other Middle Age and scholastic theologians such as Benedict of Aniane, John Scotus Erigna, Anselm, Abelard, and Albertus Magnus working from a position of commitment to the Aristotelian description of being, appear to have resorted to Aristotelianism as the best medium for articulating the Trinity for their audiences. We can borrow so much from their achievement. As a result of their commitment to communicating the truth of the God they had come to know in Christ, the Trinity was preserved and today we can talk of re-interpreting it for our own situations using the instrument of intellectual infrastructures that fit the communication needs of our own audiences.

CHAPTER 4

# God as Absolute Subject

## 4.1 Beginnings of Self-Consciousness

Western society went through a major paradigmatic change so that, by the time of Bacon and Descartes, radical anthropocentrism was deeply entrenched and philosophy in these societies no longer addressed being, substance, or essence as the basis of existence or "first cause without being caused." Instead it addressed "ideas" and the connection between the reality of the ideas and the subject, "I," who holds the ideas. This became known as Idealism. German idealism was a philosophical movement in Germany in the late eighteenth and early nineteenth centuries. It developed out of the work of Immanuel Kant in the 1780s and 1790s, and was closely linked both with romanticism and the revolutionary politics of the Enlightenment. The most well-known thinkers in the movement were Immanuel Kant, Johann Gottlieb Fichte, Friedrich Schelling, and Georg Wilhelm Friedrich Hegel. The other major contributors were Friedrich Heinrich Jacobi, Gottlob Ernst Schulze, Karl Leonhard Reinhold and Friedrich Schleiermacher.

Idealism concerned itself primarily with ideas and in a derivative sense with what it considered ideal. In this context, idea meant "any and every object of which any human mind is at any time aware."[1] This change of ideas not only meant change to focus on the "'copies' in the mind of objects

---

1. R. F. A. Hoernle, *Idealism as a Philosophical Doctrine* (London : Hodder and Stoughton Ltd, 1924), 3.

outside,"[2] but it also meant positing a theory of knowledge in which the subject is sure of the existence of the self, the "I"; the object of consciousness (the "idea"); and consciousness[3] itself. This phenomenon is what Idealist philosophy calls "self-consciousness."

Self-consciousness as a philosophical quest began with Descartes' *cogito ergo sum*. By this expression Descartes meant three things: (1) "I am" sure of "my own being" – the existence of himself is in this case envisioned, or the "I"; (2) he also meant the object of his consciousness – "the idea"; the external reality and the existence of a perfect being;[4] and (3) "consciousness" itself. Fichte understood "self-consciousness" in much the same way as Descartes. He called it the "the primordial, absolutely unconditioned first principle of all human knowledge."[5] Immanuel Kant developed this principle and used it to make philosophy aware of the fact that the external reality, which is the object of consciousness, is related to the nature of the "I" or the subject that knows it.

---

2. Ibid., 34.

3. The German technical term for consciousness is *Bewustsein*. *Bewustsein* indicates consciousness of an object or just intentional consciousness. The addition of the pronoun *selbst* (self) gives *selbstbewust*, which refers to consciousness, knowledge or awareness of oneself. The emphasis here is not necessarily on the I (who is conscious as contrasted to the external world of objects); rather, it is on seeing the external world of objects as the product, the possession or the mirror image of the "I" (see M. Inwood, "Hegel," in *The Blackwell Companion to Philosophy*, eds. Nicholas Bunnin and E. P. Tsui-James [Oxford: Blackwell Publishers, 1996], 61–63).

4. D. J. Butler, *Four Philosophies and Their Use in Education and Religion* (New York: Harper and Brothers Publishers, 1950), 269–270.

5. J. G. Fichte, *Science of Knowledge* (New York: Meredith, 1970), 93.

**Features of Philosophical Idealism**

The point of Kant, as he explains in his book *Critique of Pure Reason,* has the following features:

1) What, if anything, can be known *purely on the basis of reason,* in other words, is it possible to know anything independent of experience?
2) What is the nature of the *relation* between the *subject* "I" who knows and the *object* of knowledge?
3) *Transcendental conditions* are necessary and sufficient for knowledge. He argues that a transcendental condition is one that secures a *necessary* relation of subject to object of knowledge.

    He then asks: *Are there* any transcendental conditions? He believes that our knowledge is grounded on transcendental conditions. Due to these conditions, he argues; (i) we possess *truths which are neither logical nor empirical,* and (ii) we accept *transcendental proofs.*

4) On the basis of "I," the "object of my knowledge" and the "transcendental condition," he develops a *transcendental theory of knowledge*: Our knowledge is subject to, and possible only on the basis of, the transcendental conditions of: space and time; substance (the "I") and causality (ability to posit idea). This theory of knowledge has the following implications:
    a) First: Pure reason is *cognitively impotent.*
        i. Our knowledge is *restricted* to the realm of space and time; substance and causality;
        ii. All knowledge requires contributions from two separate sources: passive sensibility ("intuitions"); and active understanding ("concepts" and "judgements").
    b) Second: The *self* = "I" is the highest transcendental condition. It is the self who senses, possesses intuitions, and constructs representations; "I" must sit side by side with "my representation, idea."

> c) Third: Reality in the fullest sense is unknowable to us. This follows because our knowledge is restricted to "appearances," how "I" see things. For him, "things in themselves" left unconditioned are simply unknowable. As Kain has ably explained, "all objects are objects-of-my-consciousness they have been constituted by my consciousness and unified by my consciousness."[6]
> d) The relation between "I" and "the object" is (i) mediated through transcendental conditions, which ultimately refer back to the "I" as the supreme transcendental condition, and is (ii) therefore such as to restrict our knowledge to the "mere appearances" which compose empirical reality.
>
> Metaphysics is possible only in an "immanent," not in a "transcendent" condition.[7]

Hegel took this thought and developed it further. As he clearly writes in chapter IV of the *Phenomenology of the Spirit*, self-consciousness "has a double object: One is the immediate object . . . which however for self-consciousness has the character of a negative; and the second, *viz*, itself, which is the true essence."[8] Hegel's view of the negative, as Kain has explained, means "that in itself, the object is taken to be nothing – but a thing-for-my-consciousness. Self-consciousness takes itself to be the thing of significance. "I" is what is important and essential; the object is nothing but a thing-for-me."[9] In the words of Inwood, the external object is primarily the product, the possession, or the mirror image of the subject "I."[10]

In the theory of self-consciousness, God is understood as an Absolute Subject. God, in the mind of Descartes, as Butler explains

---

6. G. W. F. Hegel, *Phenomenology of the Spirit*, trans. A. V. Miller (Oxford: Clarendon Press, 1977), 105.

7. Ibid.

8. Ibid.

9. P. J. Kain, "Self-Consciousness, the Other and Hegel's Dialectic of Recognition," *Philosophy and Social Criticism* 24, no. 5 (1998): 106.

10. Inwood, "Hegel," 61.

was sure of his own being, but since he is equally sure that his being is imperfect and incomplete, he is convinced that there is another being beside himself which is complete and perfect. He asks what could possibly be the cause in him of this idea of perfect Being. In answering his question, he holds that imperfect being could hardly be the cause, because it is repugnant to think of a lesser causing a greater as it is to think of nothing causing something. And Descartes himself who possesses the idea, is an imperfect being. Therefore, he holds that perfect Being must exist beyond his own mind, and must be the cause of the idea of perfect Being in his mind.[11]

For Descartes this absolute subject or personality is the "perfect Being." Other Idealists called the Absolute Subject the "Self," "Universal mind," "Reality," "Reason" or "Spirit." Whatever they called the Absolute Subject, it is clear that they meant God.[12] These discussants were not Christian theologians although they had a well-documented inclination to religion. They were secular poets and thinkers who engaged in a discourse that was vogue at the time and so they saw no reason for employing the theologically restricted term *God* that was current within the Christian orthodoxy.

The basic thrust of the Idealists argument is that all subjects posit[13] themselves as objects and are conscious of this activity. God as an Absolute Subject also posits himself as an object and he is also conscious of that activity. God viewed from this perspective has far-reaching consequences for the orthodox Christian doctrine of God. In this scheme of things God the Father is understood to be the Subject; the Father externalizes himself as an

---

11. Butler, *Four Philosophies*, 269–270.

12. Nicholas of Cusa used the term *absolute* in referring to God as early as 1440. After that the term received wide acceptance as an expression for God in philosophical circles. Hegel used the term to refer to God within philosophical circles. He explained his preference for the term as arising from the fact that it was generally accepted as a philosophical expression of the concept of God, but this time the term was shorn of anthropomorphic presuppositions (Inwood, "Hegel," 27).

13. The term *posit* is from the German *setzen*, but Inwood has noted that in the philosophical usage it has been heavily influenced by the Greek *tithenai, tithesthai* ("to place," "to affirm," "to assume"). It primarily indicates the assumption or presupposition, the assertion or affirmation or simply the affirmation of (the existence of) an entity (Inwood, "Hegel," 224).

object by producing the Son; and the Holy Spirit is the self-consciousness of the Father with respect to the relationship he has with the object of his reflection; namely, the Son.[14] The Father, in this case, is the "I." In this scheme of things, "I" is the most important component. The Son is the object posited by the "I." The Holy Spirit is the consciousness itself, the transcendental condition by which the "I" is conscious of the Son.

## 4.2 Karl Barth

### Self-Revelation

Barth divides the analysis of his revealed Word into three parts: Holy Trinity, Jesus Christ and the Holy Spirit. He appears to prefer the term *self-revelation*,[15] because in his thinking, "God is . . . independent of everything that is not he. God is whether everything else is, or is not, whether it is in this way or some other. If there is something other, it cannot precede God, it cannot place God in dependence upon itself."[16] God reveals himself as the Lord, and not some "conditioned truth." For God to be known he must reveal himself, and this he decisively did in the Incarnation throughout which he remained the divine subject.[17] As such he attributes exclusiveness to the rootage of the Trinitarian doctrine in the divine self-revelation. For him, there can be no creaturely analogues, whether in the realm of nature, culture, history, religion or human psychology.[18] He cautions however against quick dismissal of these so called vestiges of the Trinity and argues that they may be useful as long as (1) their significance is understood

---

14. Inwood, "Hegel," 613–614.

15. It is important to note that these terms *self-revelation* and *self-communication* also indicate the difference between these two theologians. For Barth, the concept of self-revelation emphasizes the fact that God cannot be known except as he has revealed himself. Rahner uses self-communication to indicate what he believes is the capacity of all men to know God. Rahner's concept of self-communication would play a major role in his theology of the "anonymous Christ."

16. Karl Barth, *Church Dogmatics II: The Doctrine of God, Part 1, The Knowledge of God* (Edinburgh: T. & T. Clark, 1957), 308.

17. Karl Barth, *Church Dogmatics I: The Doctrine of the Word of God, Part 2* (Edinburgh: T. & T. Clark, 1956), 131ff; cf. *Church Dogmatics II*, Part 1, 516ff.

18. Karth Barth, *Church Dogmatics I: The Doctrine of the Word of God, Part 1* (Edinburgh: T. & T. Clark, 1955), 334–337.

in light of revelation; and (2) they are not used as another root of the doctrine.[19]

Barth begins his articulation of the doctrine of the Trinity from commitment to the position that God's revelation is "God alone, wholly God, God himself." The basic explanation of this premise is that God reveals himself as Yahweh. He alone is the revealer, and moreover, he is wholly revelation. He himself is what is revealed.[20] For Barth, "God cannot reveal anything more certain, more specific, more living than himself. Any emptiness or abstraction that we might first feel when hearing the term 'God' is on our side."[21]

## God as the Father

By God, Barth means the Father. The Father is the subject, the "I." As the "I," Barth understands the Father as the *principium* of deity.[22] For Barth, the Father's being *principium* of deity, or the divine fountain, means that he is the mode of God's "existence in which he is the originator of his other modes of existence."[23] Barth graphically describes the Father as this "thing, the type, origin, knowledge, will in God, in which he distinguishes Himself from Himself, from which proceeds the other thing, to wit the copy, outcome, word, decision; in short this fact that He can relate Himself as Creator and as our Father to one distinct from Himself outside of Him."[24] Elsewhere he talks of God as one Lord in one, not triple.[25] Unity for him is to be understood as a condition in which we have the one divine "I" three times.[26] With the view that God means the Father and that the Father is in fact the *principium* of deity, Barth reached the conclusion that God is the one personal God in the mode of the Father, in the mode of the Son and

---

19. Ibid., 338–344.
20. Barth, *Church Dogmatics I*, 87–95; J. Moltmann, *The Trinity and the Kingdom* (San Francisco: Harper and Row, 1981), 140.
21. Barth, *Church Dogmatics I*, 89.
22. Ibid., 111, 114, 119.
23. Barth, *Church Dogmatics I, Part 1*, 451.
24. Ibid., 452.
25. Ibid., 349.
26. Ibid., 351.

in the mode of the Spirit.²⁷ Notice that Barth explains in details the inappropriateness of using the term "person" in today's Trinitarian discourses. He believes that in today's world, the three *upostaseis* may have the baggage of three centers of consciousness or simply tritheism. He then proposes "mode of being."²⁸

## The Son

The following words of Barth indicate how he viewed the Son:

> If we wish to state who Jesus Christ is . . . we must also state or at least make clear – and inexorably so – that we are speaking of the Lord of Heaven and earth, who neither has nor did have any need of heaven or earth or man, who created them out of free love and according to his very own good pleasure, who adopts man, not according to the latter's merit, but according to his own mercy, not in virtue of the latter's capacity, but in virtue of his own miraculous power. He is the Lord who . . . never ceases in the very slightest to be God, who does not give his glory to another. In this, as Creator, Reconciler and Redeemer, He is a truly loving, serving God. He is the King of all kings just as when he enters into the profoundest hiddenness in "meekness of heart."²⁹

What Barth means in the above excerpt is not entirely clear until we find other places where he understands the Son as "mode" of the Father. In Barth's own words, Christ – the Word of God – meets us as the Father himself "but in another way, in a different way of being."³⁰ He is the Father's revelation and nothing more or less. The Father is wholly and utterly in His revelation that is in Jesus Christ.³¹ In Jesus Christ, the Father "sets and gives

---

27. Ibid., 359.
28. Ibid., 355–360. Note that Barth is aware that he might as well be raising a controversy by mainstreaming the idea of "modes" in theological discourse. He admits that this type of statement does not explain everything or even much. The uniqueness of God means also the mystery of God. However, "know at least what we are saying when we say" that what is at issue here is God's mystery" (Ibid., 368).
29. Barth, *Church Dogmatics I, Part 2*, 133.
30. Barth, *Church Dogmatics I, Part 1*, 498.
31. Barth, *Church Dogmatics II, Part 1*, 74–75.

to be known not something, be it the greatest and the most significant, but Himself exactly as He posits and knows Himself."[32] Elsewhere Barth describes the eternal Logos as "the eternal Word of the Father who speaks from all eternity, or the eternal thought of the Father who thinks from all eternity, the Word in which God thinks Himself, or expresses Himself by Himself."[33]

## The Holy Spirit

The Holy Spirit is understood by Barth as the eternal Lord, distinct from the Father and the Son, yet related to them as their common factor, fellowship or simply as "participation" of the Father and the Son. In that case then, He is "the common factor between the mode of existence of God the Father and God the Son, . . . What is common to them as far as they are the Father and the Son." He is the "Communion," the act of "commityness" of the Father and the Son.[34] Elsewhere he gives this "participation," "communion," and "commityness" the love flavor, so that the Father and the Son are viewed as participating in each other on the ground of love. Love, it is emphasized "is the essence of the relation between the Father and the Son."[35] The Holy Spirit in Barth's theology is therefore a correlation between the Father and the Son – the correlation being love: ". . . God is love and love is God."[36] Although the Spirit is the bond of love between the Father and the Son, he also presents the view that the Spirit emanates from both the Father and the Son. For him the *filioque* emphasizes the twofold sending of the Spirit, the fellowship of the Father and the Son and it also offers logic for creation, revelation, and reconciliation.[37]

## Perichoresis

Note however that although Barth would like to see "unity in Trinity and Trinity in unity," he believes that the term that adequately describes the

---

32. Barth, *Church Dogmatics I, Part 1*, 476.
33. Ibid., 499.
34. Ibid., 469, 527.
35. Ibid., 480.
36. Ibid., 488.
37. Ibid., 474–481.

relationship for him represents movement of the two thoughts.[38] Each of the modes is described as participating in the other two in what he sees as *perichoresis* or *circumincession*. The modes are three in distinction but not in separation.[39] All their acts are attributed to God since each of the modes is at work. This sounds very much like Augustine's *Opera Trinitatis ad extra sunt indivisa* (the external works of the Trinity are not divided) by which formula, he intended the mystery and unity of God. Appropriations or individual acts attributed to a specific mode may be spoken of as long as such talk is biblically acceptable.[40]

## 4.3 Karl Rahner

### Self-Communication

Rahner chose the term *self-communication*, because he believes in a form of self-communication of God. For him, self-communication is the root of the Trinity. This concept will also form his logic for a divinized subjective orientation in all humans. To admit a self-communicating God, argues Rahner, is to accept the possibility or a disposition to a transcendental experience of the absolute, which he also calls the "mystery, one and the nameless." As far as Rahner is concerned, we come to know God because God is a self-communicating God.[41] Consequently, for Rahner, the offer and possibility of grace is given with human nature itself.[42] He prefers to call the Son and the Holy Spirit the "two processions" or "self-communications" of God. These two are, for Rahner, mystery itself.[43] Note also that the language of self-communication in Rahner presupposes a personal recipient. Whereas Barth emphasizes man's inability to hear the word of God on account of sinfulness thus requiring the Spirit's intervention,

---

38. Ibid., 369f.
39. Ibid., 370.
40. Ibid., 372f.
41. K. Rahner, *Foundations of Christian Faith: An Introduction to the Idea of Christianity*, trans. W. V. Dych (New York: Seabury, 1978), 44, 53; cf. Rahner, *Theological Investigations* IV, 50, 106.
42. Rahner, *Foundations of Christian Faith*, 149.
43. Rahner, *Theological Investigations* IV, 72.

Rahner emphasizes that human beings have inbuilt capacity to receive God's self-communication.

For Rahner, this is possible because of what he sees as the four "double aspects" in man. He talks of the elements of our personality that move us to step beyond ourselves (past, history, offer, knowledge) and elements of our personality that reflect our openness and receptivity (future, transcendence, acceptance, love). The presence of these "double aspects" of God's self-communication allow a duality of "word and response" and "going out and return" between ourselves and God.[44] Creation for him, therefore, does not exist independent of God's self-communication, but more so as "element in that wider and more radical decision of God's will to impart himself to that which is other than himself and not divine."[45] The very presence of these "double aspects" of God's self-communication is Rahner's other way of affirming vestiges of the Trinity in human beings.

This self-communicating God has presented himself in such a way that there can never be a distinction between God as Godself (the immanent Trinity) and God as he relates to us (economic Trinity). As such, he advances the view that the immanent Trinity is the economic Trinity and the economic Trinity is the immanent Trinity.[46] For Rahner, the immanent Trinity as we have used it in our churches is not irrelevant; instead we can have new confidence and speak of "this very God himself in the strict sense."[47] He believes that in order to arrive at this position, the Christian community must once again develop interest in the Trinity. He says:

> The methodological principle is the identity of the Trinity of the economy of salvation and the immanent Trinity. . . .
> The gift which God imparts himself to the world is precisely

---

44. K. Rahner, *The Trinity* (New York: Crossroad, 1970/1997), 88ff. See also footnote 11 on the same page. Here, he admits that these aspects are not the only ones. He explains that all that is important is that they exist and as such sufficiently clarify his idea of the "doubleness of God's self-communication."

45. K. Rahner, *Theological Investigations* XI (London: Darton, Longman and Todd, 1974), 219.

46. K. Rahner, *Theological Investigations* I, trans. C. Ernest (London: Darton, Longman and Todd, 1965). See also *Theological Investigations* IV.

47. Rahner, *Foundations of Christian Faith*, 136.

God as the triune God, and not something produced by him through efficient causality, something that represents him.[48]

This axiom means that Rahner can comfortably understand God's pre-temporal identity as being identical with the economic Trinity evident in the history of salvation. In other words, the appearing of the Son and the coming of the Holy Spirit are constitutive in the identity of God. We therefore cannot conceive of the eternal identity of God without considering the Son and the Holy Spirit.[49]

## God as the Father

Whereas Rahner puts accent on the axiom, he simultaneously promotes the view that the Father is "God as such." When the term God is mentioned, what Rahner hears is the Father. And so for him, the Father is the God proper.[50] Rahner explains that,

> when the New Testament thinks of God, it is the concrete, individual, uninterchangeable Person who comes into its mind, who is in fact the Father and is called so that inversely, when it is being spoken of, it is not the single divine nature that is seen, subsisting in three hypostases, but the concrete Person who possesses the divine nature unoriginately, and communicates it by eternal generation to a Son too and by spiration to the Spirit.[51]

Elsewhere he states that in the New Testament, God signifies the Father, the Unbegotten Begetter, the font and origin of divinity (*fontalis*), who communicates the divine essence[52] through Christ and the Spirit.[53] He appears to find the *kenosis* particularly attractive for explaining this position, as Cawte explains: "In that self-emptying he posits the existence of the other. He gives himself away without loosing himself. He establishes the

---

48. K. Rahner, *Encyclopedia of Theology* (New York: Seabury, 1975), 1758.

49. C. E. Braaten, *Our Naming of God: Problems and Prospects of God-Talk Today* (Minneapolis, MN: Fortress Press, 1981), 4.

50. Rahner, *Theological Investigations*, I, 126–148.

51. Ibid., 146.

52. Rahner, *The Trinity*, 102.

53. Ibid., 16–17.

existence of the other, and retains it as his own. In retaining it as his own, he establishes it in its own genuine reality."[54] He reasons that in taking this perspective, he is in line with the early creeds, liturgical practice as well as Greek patristic theology. This approach, he believes precludes the Latin tendency to think of God's essence before the person of the Father.[55]

## The Son

He refers to Jesus interchangeably as Son, Word, Logos. Son/Word/Logos is for him God's self-communication as knowledge. He reasons that the Father expresses or communicates only by speaking his Word.[56] The Word uttered, Logos, is the knowledge whom he imparts "as his own personal self disclosure"[57] or "concrete self-disclosure."[58] The utterance and the incarnated Christ are seen here as having a necessary relationship. In Rahner's own thought, "the Word is essentially the expressible, he who can be expressed even in the non-divine, being the Word of the Father, in whom the Father can express himself and freely exteriorize himself, and because, when this takes place, that which we call human nature comes to being."[59]

For Rahner, this "exteriorizing" of the Father by the Son also means "the indissoluble, irrevocable" presence of the Father in the world as "salvation, love, and forgiveness, as communication to the world of the most intimate depths of the divine reality itself."[60] The Son/Word/Logos is the Father made visible, exteriorized, or revealed for the sake of man and his salvation. Therefore Jesus Christ is the Father as he reveals himself.

## The Holy Spirit

In this scheme of things, the Holy Spirit is understood to be the mutual love that exists between the Father and his Logos or, put in another way, the love between the Father and his exterior self.[61] He simply is that deep

---

54. John Cawte, "Karl Rahner's Conception of God's Self Communication to Man," *Heythrop Journal* 25 (1984): 268.
55. Rahner, *The Trinity*, 16–18, 83–84.
56. Rahner, *Theological Investigations* IV, 93.
57. Rahner, *Theological Investigations* I, 96.
58. Ibid., 100.
59. Ibid., 93.
60. Ibid., 49.
61. Ibid., 96.

intimacy and fondness that the Father has for his Logos and which the Logos has for the Father. He sees a universal work of the Spirit which for him means a chance for salvation for everyone: "If there can be a faith which is creative of salvation among non-Christians, and if it may be hoped that in fact it is found on a large scale, then it is to be taken for granted that this faith is made possible and is based upon the supernatural grace of the Spirit."[62]

## Ordering the Modes

Rahner discusses the ordering of the two processions,[63] but he doesn't quite give an adequate account of this ordering.[64] He accepts the *filioque*[65] although it appears this doctrine is not central to Rahner's argumentation. Battaglia commenting on this, notes:

> This is not surprising given that Rahner rejects the psychological analogy of the Trinity. . . . This has resulted in Trinitarian scholars in the Rahnerian tradition ignoring the Filioque, rejecting it altogether, or replacing it with a Spirituque (Son proceeding from the Father and the Spirit). In this way the Filioque either is asserted a mere fact without explanation, or is regarded as unimportant.[66]

Like Barth, Rahner rejects "person" language in the Trinity, he however retains "substance," "essence" and "relation." He argues that the words he retained carry "logical explanations" (explanations that use words to make the meaning of something precise) and therefore can become unchangeable dogma; whereas "person" belongs to the class of ontic explanations (explanations that use a state of affairs to explain the meaning of something) and is therefore unacceptable.[67] Like Barth, he argues that the term "person" has

---

62. Rahner, *Foundations of Christian Faith*, 316.
63. Rahner, *The Trinity*, 83, 106, 112, 116–117.
64. N. Omerald, "Wrestling with Rahner on the Trinity," *Irish Theological Quarterly* 68 (2003): 220–224.
65. Rahner, *The Trinity*, 66, 83, 117.
66. Vincent Battaglia, "An Examination of Karl Rahner's Trinitarian Theology," *Australian E-Journal of Theology* 9, no. 1 (March 2007): 10.
67. Rahner, *The Trinity*, 51–56, 69, 73.

acquired new meanings since its use in magisterial teaching and as such it has become inappropriate:

> Nonetheless, the main difficulty regarding the concept of person in the doctrine of the Trinity is rather different, and we have already mentioned it several times before now: When *today we* speak of person in the plural, we think almost necessarily, because of the modern meaning of the word, of several spiritual centers of activity, of several subjectivities and liberties. But there are not three of these in God – not only because in God there is only *one* essence, hence one absolute self-presence, but also because in God there is only one self-utterance of the Father, the Logos. The Logos is not the one who utters, but the one who is uttered. And there is properly no *mutual* love between Father and Son, for this would presuppose two acts. But there is a loving self-acceptance of the Father (and of the Son, because of knowledge and love), and this self-acceptance gives rise to the distinction. Of course, that which we call "three persons" in God exist in God with self-awareness. There is in God a knowledge of these three persons (hence in each person about himself and about the two other persons), a knowledge about the Trinity both *as consciousness* and as "*object*" of knowledge. But there are not three consciousness; rather, the one consciousness subsists in a threefold way. There is only one real consciousness in God, which is shared by Father, Son, and Spirit, by each in his own proper way. Hence the threefold subsistence is not qualified by three consciousnesses. The "subsistence" itself is as such not "personal," if we understand this word in the modern sense. The "distinctness" of the persons is not constituted by a distinctness of conscious subjectivities, nor does it include the latter. This distinctness is conscious. However, it is not conscious for three subjectivities, but it is the awareness of this distinction in one only real consciousness.[68]

---

68. Ibid., 106–107.

In the thought of Rahner, therefore, we find a one subject God who refuses to be expressed in the classical Nicene terms of "One Substance" and "Three Persons." Instead, Rahner proposes that God be understood as one subject and three distinct modes or relative ways in which God subsists.[69] To sum up: "The one and the same God is given for us as Father, Son-Logos, and Holy Spirit, or the Father gives himself in absolute self-communication through the Son in the Holy Spirit."[70] As far as Rahner is concerned, *person* should mean "that which subsists as distinct in a rational nature"[71] or put differently, "distinct manner of subsisting."[72] He takes note of the doctrine of appropriations (or proper roles) and redefines it to what he calls "quasi-formal causality" by which he means that "each divine person possesses its own proper relation to some created reality."[73]

## 4.4 Renown Theologians in the Model

It appears that the Protestant theology has been more generous to the "God as Absolute Subject" model than the Catholics. Karl Barth has had a battalion of epigones who have seen no reason not to identify with his revelational positivism. Some of the well-known theologians heavily influenced by Karl Barth's formulation of the doctrine of the Trinity are Eberhard Jüngel, T. H. L. Parker, Robert Jenson and Thomas Forsyth Torrance. Apart from these Barthians, Idealist theology is a strong feature of the works of Tillich, Brunner, Bultmann, Thielicke, Bonhoeffer and Niebuhr. Paul Tillich, for instance, constructs his idea of the Trinity from the position that life is dialectical, it is a movement of separation and return and that dialectic in fact determines all life processes including divine life.[74] The Father is the depth, the unknown.[75] Depth becomes form, also the Logos, the known

---

69. Rahner, *Theological Investigations* I, 95–96; cf. Rahner, *The Trinity*, 103ff.
70. K. Rahner quoted in Moltmann, *The Trinity and the Kingdom*, 147.
71. Rahner, *The Trinity*, 104 n.25.
72. Ibid., 111–113.
73. Ibid., 77.
74. Paul Tillich, *Systematic Theology*, vols. I, II, III (Chicago: The University of Chicago Press, 1951, 1957, 1963), II:90; cf. III:284.
75. Tillich, *Systematic Theology* I, 286f.

side of God.[76] The Spirit according to this conception is the unity of the two.[77] On the basis of his understanding of the Spirit, Tillich would simply say God is spirit.[78]

In the context of Catholicism, it suffices to say that the influence of Rahnerian theology appears to be primarily a German affair. In the USA, it is mainly among some Jesuit enclaves in the Hispanics and the Anglo Americans. But even in these contexts, Rahner's influence comes second to Ignatius. In Africa, Rahner has very little significance. African Catholicism is largely Aquinian in its theology. Some of the scholars who have found Rahner's patterns innovative are David Coffey and Gavin D'Costa.

## 4.5 Conclusion

I see the remarkable achievements of both Barth and Rahner attributable to two processes. One is their mastery of the organizing principle; namely the observation that the doctrine of the Trinity which they see as the guardian of the right faith has suffered untold neglect and as such the Christians have turned out be mere "monotheists" who are disturbingly ignorant of the centrality of the incarnation and the significance of the Holy Spirit in the Christian economy. This mastery of the organizing principle also explains the passion they both demonstrate in presenting the thesis: *The Economic Trinity is the Immanent Trinity and the Immanent Trinity is the Economic Trinity.* The other, of course, is the ease and fluency with which they seem to use the instrument of German idealism as a media for their theological conversations. Their argumentations rotate around the "I," the "object of my knowledge" and the "transcendental condition," or put in other way "thesis," "antithesis," "synthesis" with so much ease that an untrained mind would hardly recognise their Idealistic bent.

---

76. Ibid., 250f.
77. Ibid., 156.
78. Ibid., 249.

CHAPTER 5

# God as Community in Unity

## 5.1 Apophaticism

The existential character of the mystical experience is the platform from which the Orthodox Christian theology operates. Two concepts are important for our thrust into the Eastern mystical experience: apophaticism and uncreated energies – these two doctrines must be seen together as two sides of the same coin. Eastern theology sees apophaticism not as their innovation but as a heritage they have gladly received from the church fathers in their struggle to steer the church away from what Lossky calls "the trinity of Plotinus." Lossky sees in this counterfeit "three consubstantial hypostases: the One, the Intelligence, and the Soul of the world. Their consubstantiality does not rise to the Trinitarian antinomy of Christian dogma: it appears as a descending hierarchy and realizes itself through the ceaseless flow of the hypostases which pass the one into the other, reciprocally reflecting each other."[1]

If the immanent Trinity was "wombed," so to speak, in the context of apophaticism, then as Eastern theology[2] argues, it must form the context within which Trinity discourses are done. Lossky believes:

> The mystery of the Trinity only becomes accessible to that ignorance which rises above all that can be contained within the

---

1. Lossky, *The Mystical Theology*, 49.
2. Note that Eastern theology is today being discussed within the framework of the Russian School and the Neopatristic School. Whereas they all agree on apophaticism, the Russian school is more charitable to new philosophy, especially Sophiology.

concepts of the philosophers. Yet this *ignorantia*, not only *docta* but charitable also, re-descends again upon these concepts that it may mould them; that it may transform the expressions of human wisdom into the instruments of that Wisdom of God which is to the Greeks foolishness. It required the superhuman efforts of an Athanasius of Alexandria, of a Basil, of a Gregory Nazianzen and of many others, to purify the concepts of Hellenistic thought, to break down the watertight bulkheads by the introduction of a Christian apophaticism which transformed rational speculation into a contemplation of the mystery of the Trinity.[3]

Apophaticism or negative theology (because it rejects philosophy as opposed to kataphaticism or positive theology because it sees sense in the use of philosophy) in its right context is not "necessarily a theology of ecstasy. It is, above all, an attitude of mind which refuses to form concepts about God." This attitude, Lossky explains, "utterly excludes all abstract and purely intellectual theology which would adapt the mysteries of the wisdom of God to human ways of thoughts."[4] Eastern Christianity believes that apophaticism negates all definitions and creatively attributes anthropomorphism where it belongs, holding that the otherness of which requires incomprehensibility was the only safe knowledge about God.[5] God is beyond all human and logical categories and divine essence totally transcends knowledge and comprehension in this life and the next. In the thought of Fr Sergius Bulgakov, apophatic theology, "acquires the significance of an epistemological barrier and corrective to all positive theology."[6] It respects the mystery of the *how* of God. In this sense therefore, all theology must strive to be apophatic.[7]

---

3. Lossky, *The Mystical Theology*, 49.

4. Ibid., 39.

5. John D. Zizioulas, "The Teaching of the 2nd Council on the Holy Spirit in Historical and Ecumenical Perspective," in *Credo in Spiritum Sanctum*, vol. 1, ed. J. S. Martins (Rome: Libreria Editrice Vaticana, 1983), 40.

6. Sergius Bulgakov, *The Comforter*, trans. Boris Jakim (Grand Rapids: Eerdmans, 2004), 362.

7. Note however that this position while dominant in the Neopatristic School is currently contested in the Russian School. This school birthed in the context of displaced

> **Basic Qualities of Aphophaticism**
>
> In apophaticism, we see at least three closely knit strands:
> 1) Emphasis on the existential attitude, the experience thus engagement of the whole man – his theology and his spirituality. No separation between the static (theology taking place within the dogmatic confines of the "static" Church) *vis-à-vis* the dynamic (capacity to rise to spiritual heights unattainable by the rigid ecclesiastical theologians) in religion; instead theology and mysticism "support and complete each other."[8]
> 2) The goal of the Christian is to change, to become a new man, to attain "union with God" (*theôsis*):
>    a) Our participation in the divine nature is mediated through and by God's energies;
>    b) Humanity will come to share in the divine nature but not in the same manner as the Trinity;
>    c) We do not attain this kind of participation because we remain free beings, possessing our own unique nature
> 3) Humanity, therefore, must not confine itself to a single way of gaining access to God; instead, the mystical and the dogmatic are united through the reception of "the unceasing revelation of the Holy Spirit in the Church."[9]

## 5.2 The Divine Energies

Then there is the doctrine of the "uncreated energies." These energies (*energeiai*) are said to proceed from the Godhead. By contemplating the

---

Christian communities are more charitable to philosophy, especially Sophiology. The Russian School is represented by Sergius Bulgakov. In his book, *The Comforter* (p. 362), Bulgakov examines the apophatic tradition from Plato to Jacob Boehme and details his own kataphatic theology in *Svet neverchernii* [*The Unfading Light*] (Moscow: Izdatel'stvo 'Respublika,' 1994). For him, the "NO of apophatic theology is connected with a certain kataphatic YES" (p. 360).

8. Lossky, *The Mystical Theology*, 8.
9. Ibid., 236.

function and purpose of the energies in bestowing grace upon humanity, and in revealing something of the essence of God in and through his created order, human beings gain a glimpse of their future deified state when they become "partakers of the divine nature." Lossky carefully notes three important things for our attention: (1) That our participation in the divine nature is mediated through and by God's energies; (2) Humanity will come to share in the divine nature but not in the same manner as the Trinity. Explaining this, Lossky says: "Even though we share the same human nature as Christ and receive in Him the name of sons of God, we do not ourselves become the divine hypostasis of the Son by the fact of the Incarnation. We are unable, therefore, to participate in either the essence or the hypostases of the Holy Trinity";[10] (3) We do not attain this kind of participation because although we are God's creatures created for participating in the divine fullness, preserved, granted grace, and guided towards the final goal, in the interim we remain free beings, possessing our own unique nature.[11] Elsewhere, Lossky explains this as follows:

> The personal character of a human being who has entered on the way to union is never impaired, even though he renounces his own will and his natural inclinations. It is just by this free renunciation of all by which nature belongs to it that the human personality comes to its full realization in grace. What is not free and definitely conscious has no personal value.[12]

On the other hand, lest it be misconstrued, Lossky warns that the ecstasy (*ekstasis*) experienced by the mystic is not an end in itself; instead, it is but a stepping stone to a constant participation in divine life. The emphasis again falls on the fact that for God's grace to abound, the will of the human being must cooperate with the will of God. This the human person must do freely and with complete consciousness of his continual experience of and proximity to the divine life.[13]

---

10. Ibid., 70.
11. Ibid., 88–89.
12. Ibid., 217.
13. Ibid., 199.

## 5.3 God as Father, Son and Holy Spirit

If one speaks of God it is always, for the Eastern Church, in the concrete – Father, Son and Holy Spirit. Each of the three hypostases are united in an indissoluble bond of one nature in a manner that is not only proper to it but which also distinguishes one hypostasis from the other two. The Eastern theology wishes to situate the Trinity discourse in the context of the meeting point between Christianity, Judaism and Greek religions for there in the crisis of her identity, God – Father, Son and Holy Spirit – was revealed. Lossky has noted this in the lines of St Gregory Nazianzen when he says:

> When I say *God*, I mean Father, Son and Holy Ghost; for Godhead is neither diffused beyond these, so as to introduce a multitude of gods, nor yet bounded by a smaller compass than these, so as to condemn us for a poverty-stricken conception of deity, either Judaizing to save the monarchy, or falling into Hellenism by the multitude of our gods.[14]

But what is even more dazzling to Lossky is what appears to be an apophatic experience that accompanied St Gregory Nazianzen's theologizing when he speaks in his Oration on Baptism:

> No sooner do I conceive of the One than I am illumined by the splendour of the Three; no sooner do I distinguish them than I am carried back to the One. When I think of any One of the Three, I think of Him as the whole, and my eyes are filled, and the greater part of what I am thinking of escapes me. I cannot grasp the greatness of that One so as to attribute a greater greatness to the rest. When I contemplate the Three together, I see but one torch, and cannot divide or measure out the undivided light.[15]

In this excerpt, we see not only a classic display of the three in their concreteness but also what is clearly a mark of an apophatic theologizing in St Gregory Nazianzen who, though a philosopher wishing to address a

---

14. St Gregory Nazianzen, "Oratio XLV, 4," P.G., XXXVI, 628 C.
15. St Gregory Nazianzen, "Oratio XL, 41," P.G., XXXVI, 417 BC.

technical audience, rises above rational concepts and darts back and forth in pursuit of the one and the three in order to attain *theosis*.[16] Lossky, in fact, seizes this opportunity to bring to fore once again the Orthodox dogma of apophaticism and *theosis*. He sees the Orthodox Church's defense of the mystery of God who is personal and yet not a person as linked fundamentally to *theosis* which is the benefit wrought by contemplating on the mystery. When one contemplates this mystery, Lossky pontificates, the human soul gets lifted "beyond the world of being, changing and confused, in bestowing upon it this stability in the midst of passions; this serenity, or *apatheia*, which is the beginning of deification."[17] He repeats the same admonition elsewhere where he reminds his readers once again of the transformative power of contemplation on the Holy Trinity: "The perfecting of gnosis is the contemplation of the divine light of the Holy Trinity; that full consciousness which is the parousia, the judgement, and the entering into eternal life, being fulfilled here and now . . . before death and the resurrection, in the saints who live in uninterrupted communion with God."[18]

This model of the Trinity distinguishes the three hypostases only by their origin: "The Father, the Son, and the Holy Ghost are one in all respects save those of being unbegotten, of filiation and of procession."[19] This apophatic line of argumentation, preserved in the works of St John Damascene, proves useful in conveying the idea: "For in their hypostatic or personal properties alone, the properties of being unbegotten, of filiation and of procession – do the three divine hypostases differ from each other, being indivisibly divided, not by essence but by the distinguishing mark of their proper and peculiar hypostasis."[20] However for a neat summation of the distinction between the hypostatic characteristics, Eastern theology refers to St Gregory Nazianzen's position:

> The very fact of being unbegotten, or begotten, or proceeding, has given the name of Father to the First, of the Son to the Second, and to the Third, Him of whom we are speaking, of the

---

16. Lossky, *The Mystical Theology*, 46.
17. Ibid., 48.
18. Ibid., 247.
19. St John Damascene quoted in Lossky, *The Mystical Theology*, 54.
20. Ibid.

Holy Ghost, that the distinction of the Three Hypostases may be preserved in the one nature and dignity of the Godhead. For neither is the Son Father, for the Father is One, but He is what the Father is; nor is the Spirit Son because He is of God, for the Only-begotten is One, but He is what the Son is. The Three are One in Godhead, and the One Three in properties; so that neither is the Unity a Sabellian one, nor does the Trinity countenance the present evil division. (i.e. Arianism)[21]

## 5.4 Hypostases Exist in *Perichoresis*

Eastern theology sees the need for a reconfiguration of "person" in today's Trinity discourse. Lossky for instance sees a major difference in how the term person is used in today's conversations and its specialized usage in the formulation of the dogma. Zizioulas does a similar thing in his very elaborate discourse which he calls the "ontology of person" which was a philosophical landmark in the church fathers' quest for the language of the Trinity.[22] Human persons or hypostases as they obtain in today's dispensation, Lossky argues, are not only isolated but they also "do not exist the one within the other"; while, "in the Holy Trinity it is quite the reverse . . . the hypostases dwell in one another."[23] To the extent that the human persons are isolated, their works are also distinct. This however is not the case with the divine Persons since the Three have one nature, "a single will, a single power, a single operation."[24] The divine Persons dwell in one another in a *koinōnia*, in perichoretic manner. St John Damascene explaining this says:

> The persons are made one not so as to commingle, but so as to cleave to each other, and they have their being in each other (*ten en allelais perichoresin echousi*) without any coalescence or commingling. Nor do the Son and Spirit stand apart, nor are they sundered in essence as in the heresy of Arius. For, to put

---

21. St Gregory Nazianzen, "Oratio XXXI (Theologica V), ix" P.G., XXXVI, 144 A.
22. John D. Zizioulas, *Being as Communion: Studies in the Personhood of the Church* (Crestwood, NY: St Vladimir's Seminary Press, 1985), 36.
23. St John Damascene quoted in Lossky, *The Mystical Theology*, 53.
24. Lossky, *The Mystical Theology*, 53.

it concisely, the Godhead is undivided; and it is just like three suns cleaving to each other without separation, and giving out light mingled and conjoined into one . . . Each one of the persons contains the unity by this relation to the others no less than by this relation to Himself.[25]

The apophatic argumentation admits distinction in the divine Persons but is clearly unfavorable to the manner of divine processions: "The mode of generation and the mode of procession are incomprehensible, . . . We have learned that there is a difference between generation and procession, but the nature of the difference we in no wise understand."[26] Eastern theology sees this apophatic attitude in St Gregory Nazianzen who rejected the attempts to define the mode of the divine procession:

> You ask, what is the procession of the Holy Spirit? Do you tell me first what is the unbegottenness of the Father, and I will then explain to you the physiology of the generation of the Son, and the procession of the Spirit, and we shall both of us be stricken with madness for prying into the mystery of God.[27]

Elsewhere St Gregory Nazianzen continuing the same apophatic pontification says: "You hear that there is generation? Do not waste your time in seeking after the how. You hear that the Spirit proceeds from the Father? Do not busy yourself about the how."[28]

## 5.5 The Filioquism versus Monopatrism

The "God as Community" model sees the issue of *filioque* as a matter of philosophical speculation with neither theological merit nor apophatic value. Their argument is that the hypostases of Trinity as it stands today has adequately been distinguished by their origin: the Son is begotten, the Holy Spirit *proceeds* from the Father. The Russian School, while generally favorable to the *filioque*, they are of the opinion that the whole debate on

---

25. St John Damascene quoted in Lossky, *The Mystical Theology*, 53, 54.
26. Ibid., 54–55.
27. St Gregory Nazianzen, "Oratio XXXI (Theologica V), 8," P.G., XXXVI, 141 B.
28. St Gregory Nazianzen, "Oratio XX, ii," P.G., XXXV, 1077 C.

procession which unfortunately divided the church shouldn't have been entertained in the first place.

Father Sergius Bulgakov gives his candid critique of this process as follows in his book *The Comforter*. First, he thinks it was pointless to construct an entire dogmatic position to justify what he calls an "erroneous theologoumenon." Second, he considers it ridiculous that the whole affair received the "the seal of papal infallibility." Third, he believes "*there does not yet exist a definitive dogma of the procession of the Holy Spirit*, either with regard to the meaning of the procession or with regard to its mode." Fourth, he argues that "in and of itself, *the Filioque is not a heresy*" and as such is not a threat to the unity of the church. Fifth, he proposes the jettison of any notion of origination from the doctrine of the Trinity; that way the formulas describing the procession of the Holy Spirit "can and must be understood . . . not as mutually contradictory or mutually exclusive expressions but as equivalent in some sense." Sixth, he observes that the Western and Eastern churches in fact "do not differ in their veneration of the Holy Spirit," and what separated the churches was really a "schismatic spirit," not a dogmatic or living heresy.[29] Bulgakov thus believes that the entire dogma on the Holy Spirit needs review alongside what he considers to be the unacceptable split within the communion of the church.

This model's rejection of the *filioque* is linked to their understanding of the *monarkhia*, which for them presents the Father not only more concretely and more personally but also as the Principle of the other hypostases. The Father then is understood within the construct of *monopatrism*. Bulgakov, focusing on the need for a more personal One, argues, "the rather formalistic patristic term *ousia* is not very expressive"[30] and challenges us "to envision the divine nature 'not just as power and depth, but as self-manifesting content.'"[31] Valliere adds, quoting Bulgakov,

> ". . . if we view *ousia* only under the aspect of *personal* being, for all practical purposes we eliminate it." This is bad theology because it makes God "poorer than created spirit," construing

---

29. Bulgakov, *The Comforter*, 144–149.

30. Paul Valliere, *Modern Russian Theology: Bukharev, Soloviev, Bulgakov: Orthodox Theology in a New Key* (Edinburgh: T. & T. Clark, 2000), 333.

31. Ibid.

his personhood as "an empty, abstract ego rather than as a vital spirit with a nature of its own."[32]

For Bulgakov, God's nature is not merely subsumed into the hypostatic life but is a subsistent, personal entity, the Father.

## 5.6 The Father as *Monarkhia*

As the Principle of the other hypostases, the Father, who is a personal entity, is understood to be laying down the hypostases' relations of origin – generation and procession. Again here, Eastern theology finds resonance with St Athanasius' position: "There is a single principle of the Godhead, whence there is strictly a monarchy."[33] Lossky sees this as the basis for the Greek fathers saying, "A single God because a single Father."[34] Unity of the nature is to recognize the Godhead, the Monarchy or simply the Father.[35] St Basil notes one exception of the Father's hypostasis; that he is the "Father, and has His subsistence from no cause; and by this note again He is Himself peculiarly recognized."[36] Put differently by St Gregory Nazianzen, the Son and the Spirit are portrayed as "two new suns" together inseparable in their showing forth of the Father.[37]

For Bulgakov, the first hypostasis, the Father, represents

> . . . the transcendental principle within the Holy Trinity, he who does not reveal himself but is revealed insofar as he is immanent in the other hypostases which reveal him. He is . . . the divine subject . . . which manifests itself in the predicate. He constitutes the divine depth and mystery. He represents . . . that speechless silence which is presupposed by the Word . . . He is the primal will . . . He is the source of all beauty . . .

---

32. Ibid.
33. St Athanasius, "Contra Arianos, Oratio IV, i," P.G, XXVI, 468 B.
34. Lossky, *The Mystical Theology*, 58.
35. St Gregory Nazianzen, "Oratio XXXI (Theologica V), 14," P.G., XXXVI, 148D–149A.
36. St Basil, "Epist. XXXVIII, 4," P.G., XXXII, 329 C&#150;332 A.
37. St Gregory Nazianzen, "Oratio XXXI, 32," P.G., XXXVI, 169 B.

He is love . . . He is the Father, the source of being and of love, that love which cannot but diffuse itself.[38]

Note a mixture of apophatic theology and kataphatic theology in Bulgakov. Although his representation here is fairly kataphatic, he is simply saying that the Father is the absolute source and will of the Godhead who is revealed by the Son and the Spirit.

The Orthodox theology is quick to point out that the principle of *monarkhia* has no diminishing effect on the other hypostases. Again Eastern theology sees a clear clarification of this in the works of St Gregory Nazianzen: "I should like to call the Father the greater, because from Him flow both the equality and the being of the equals . . . but I am afraid to use the word Origin, lest I should make Him the Origin of inferiors, and thus insult Him by precedencies of honour. For the lowering of those who are from Him is no glory to the Source."[39] He repeats the same sentiment elsewhere:

> Godhead . . . neither increased nor diminished by superiorities or inferiorities; in every respect equal, in every respect the same; just as the beauty and the greatness of the heavens is one; the infinite connaturality of Three Infinite Ones, each God when considered in Himself; as the Father so the Son, as the Son so the Holy Ghost; the Three, one God when contemplated together; each God because consubstantial; the Three, one God because of the monarchy.[40]

## 5.7 Renown Theologians in the Model

Some of the renowned theologians outside Eastern Europe and Russia who have found this model favorable are J. Moltmann, Pannenberg, and Leonardo Boff. These theologians argue that any Trinity discourse must

---

38. Sergei Bulgakov, *Sophia: The Wisdom of God,* trans. Rev Patrick Thompson, Rev O. Fielding Clarke and Miss Xenia Braikevitc (Hudson: Lindisfarne Press, 1993), Rev. ed. of *The Wisdom of God: A Brief Summary of Sophiology* (New York: The Paisley Press, 1937), 38–39.

39. St Gregory Nazianzen, "In sanct. bapt. *Oratio* XL, 43," P.G., XXXVI, 419 B. 41 Ibid., 41, 417 B.

40. St Gregory Nazianzen, "In sanct. bapt. *Oratio* XL, 43," P.G., XXXVI, 41, 417 B.

begin with the revelation attested to it in Scripture.[41] They dismiss Barth's idea of revelation as derived not from what is attested in the Bible but instead it is taken from the Hegelian idea of self-revelation.[42] Once this is done, they argue, the discourse immediately switches to Trinity. For them, what needs explaining is the One. In discussing the One, they avoid philosophy and instead they turn to what they see of revelation. For them, Jesus is the revelation of God because he implements the rule of God in a way that implies the existence of God. In other words, the history of Jesus viewed from the point of view of his ministry revealed the Father.[43] Consequently, Pannenberg is able to argue on the one hand that "God's being and existence cannot be conceived apart from his rule" and on the other hand that the eternal Trinity is the basis of economic Trinity.[44]

Leonardo Boff sees in the model a pattern for dealing with some of the most persistent forms of Trinitarian heresies and the many injustices facing the global South. For him, beginning with the One inevitably leads to a doctrine of the Trinity tinged either by subordinationism (the heresy of the East) or modalism (the heresy of the West). Moreover, he argues, it justifies every form of authoritarianism, paternalism, tyranny, or autonomous individualism in political, economic, ecclesiastical, sexual, and familial relationships. For Boff, as for Pannenberg, where we begin is of pragmatic significance. He reasons that beginning with the self-revelation of God as Father, Son, and Holy Spirit, allows us to know the true God whose inner being (immanent Trinity) as well as outward activity (economic Trinity) is the unity of communion. For him, this view of God leads to a vision of human society in the image of God that on every level is marked by unity in diversity, individuality realized in relatedness, community that includes rather than excludes, mutual giving and receiving that rejects all domination and control, dependency and inferiority.[45]

---

41. Moltmann, *The Trinity and the Kingdom*, 64–65.

42. Wolfhart Pannenberg, *Systematic Theology*, 3 Vols., trans Geoffrey W. Bromiley (Grand Rapids, MI: Eerdmans, 1991–1998), I: 296.

43. Ibid., I: 310.

44. Wolfhart Pannenberg, *Theology and the Kingdom of God*, ed. Richard John Neuhaus (Philadelphia: Westminster Press, 1977), 55; cf. Pannenberg, *Systematic Theology*, II:22.

45. Leonardo Boff, *Trinity and Society* (Maryknoll, NY: Orbis Books, 1988).

David Tracy, on the other hand, has begun to see this model as having features that are of great significance to the postmodernistic world. He is particularly attracted to the apophatic and the apocalyptic formulations. When asked in an interview how he thinks about God in apophatic and apocalyptic terms, he has the following to say:

> I begin with the categories of the "void" and the "open." I am persuaded to think about God not simply in modern terms but in terms of the categories of faith. When you talk about God you are talking about two "impossible" options. Lucretius and Nietzsche talk about the void, but there is no one better on the subject than Luther. History is apocalyptic for him. It is a series of openings into the abyss. Nature is that too. The "void" has to do with experiences of extreme suffering, injustice, terror, despair or alienation.
>
> And there is no one better than the apophatic mystics with respect to regarding God as "open." I first called this category the "gracious void" but realized this was too Christian a term. So I use the term "the open." The experience of the open happens when you "let go." That's why Buddhism is such an attraction to so many contemporary people, including postmodern thinkers. It's the "let-go" aspect of faith. Even Aristotle speaks of the mystery of religion as a genuine experience.

The experience of "the open" either happens or it doesn't – or it can happen suddenly – but spiritual disciplines can prepare you for it. The "open" has to do with experiences of the sheer giftedness of life – the sense of awe and wonder one might have about the beauty of the natural world or the sheer happiness one might find in human relationships.[46]

---

46. Lois Malcolm, "An Interview with David Tracy." Lois Malcolm teaches theology at Luther Seminary in St Paul. This article appeared in *The Christian Century* (13–20 February 2002): 24–30. Accessed on http://www.religion-online.org/showarticle.asp?title=2269 on 11 May 2009.

## 5.8 Conclusion

"God as Community in Unity" is a reminder of the pre-Nicene and Nicene discourses that led to the Trinitarian formula. It appears that theology in our generation is going to increasingly focus on this period on account of "New Perspectives on Paul." The model also offers patterns that are very useful to the new heartlands of Christianity where there are a number of social concerns and the need for ecclesiologies structured around *koinonia*. Social Trinitarians have used these patterns very profitably. The model however takes Western theology to fairly unfamiliar grounds. For instance the discourse introduces apophaticism, divine energies, *theosis* and new directions on the *filioque*. These are new things to Western theology, but they must form part of the theological agenda of the global Christianity because Christianity wherever it is found is all about God.

CHAPTER 6

# God as Nyasaye

## 6.1 The Great Distractions: Tylor's Animism and Missionary Theologizing

African theology has lost a lot of time revising the stereotype image it received in the West. My book, *The Doctrine of God in African Christian Thought*,[1] has an entire section dedicated to the extensive and well-argued writings of Bolaji Idowu, J. S. Mbiti and Gabriel Satilaone. These premier African theologians directed their efforts to the unfortunate nineteenth-century religious propaganda, *animism*,[2] whose chief architect E. B. Tylor used the privilege of academic learning and the support of the vogue expansionist mentality to engrave it illegibly in the memory of mission agencies. From that time, in the mission circles (and it was not better in other circles as well), the view of Africans as animists determined how mission was going to be done in Africa. It needs to be remembered that Africa (read African religions) was not represented at the World Missionary Conference held in Edinburgh, Scotland, in 1910 on the theme "Missionary Problems in Relation to the non-Christian World." At that conference, four world religions were represented: religions of China, religions of Japan, Islam, and Hinduism. And so whatever conclusions were arrived at – whether positive or negative – Africa would perhaps simply be an object, a giant

---

1. J. H. O. Kombo, *The Doctrine of God in African Christian Thought* (Leiden: Brill, 2007).

2. E. B. Tylor, *Primitive Culture: Researches into Development of Mythology, Philosophy, Religion, Language, Art, and Custom* (New York: Holt, 1889).

religious *tabula rasa* which would be filled from the scratch with content from missions abroad.

In fact, in the Edinburgh's World Missionary Conference (1910) conference's report chapter titled "The Church in the Mission Field as an Evangelistic Agency," one gets the impression that it is all about the missionary:

> The small native Church, left to itself, is in danger within a generation or two of losing its tone under the influence of monotony, isolation, or ill-success. As a rule it needs the guidance and stimulus of the spiritual ideas, as well as the spiritual aids, which are supplied through contact by means of missionaries with the life of older Churches. While many noble leaders have arisen among the early converts in the field, it will take time to develop a sufficient number of men of knowledge, gifts, and character to enable the Church to stand with advantage, or even with safety, apart from foreign missionaries.[3]

And so the factors that would be considered in evangelizing Africa, how and where the missionaries were to be deployed, what methods to be used in mission task, as well as the essential nature of the spiritual disciplines were all going to depend on the missionary. Missionary theologizing would take its cue from here. George Kinoti, in his book, *Hope for Africa*, illustrates what this ultimately came to:

> There is a sense in which Christianity in Africa is the white man's religion. The denominations we belong to, the liturgies we use, the hymns we sing, the theologies which govern our beliefs and conduct, be they liberal or evangelical, are all made in the West. Most of the Christian books we read originate from the West and are usually written for Western readers. This is not to blame the Western church: it is time to say to

---

3. World Missionary Conference 1910, Report of Commission I: *Carrying the Gospel to All the Non-Christian World* (Edinburgh: Oliphant, Anderson and Ferrier, 1910), 342. See also Andrew F. Walls, "The Great Commission 1910-2010," Lecture delivered at the University of Edinburgh, 2002. Accessed on http://www.towards2010.org.uk/downloads/t2010paper01walls.pdf on 8 May 2009.

the African Christians to begin to think and do things for themselves.[4]

Africa therefore has essentially had no theology, except that of their respective denominations. And so if Africa has had no independent theology, then in the context of our present discussion, we have had the western Augustinian-Aquinian axis of the Trinity, which for many was the untranslatable magisterium of the missionary century par excellence.[5]

Ecclesial cartographers are today agreed that since the end of the colonial era in the 1960s and 1970s, African Christianity has registered a phenomenal expansion. Philip Jenkins in his book, *The New Faces of Christianity* (2006), is clearly more optimistic. This expansion however has been attributed to three things: (1) access to the vernacular translations of Scriptures; (2) the rise of independency, Pentecostalism and the charismatic movements; and (3) unhindered operation of local lay evangelists and catechists. What this means is that the Christianity that is growing in Africa and that we read about in Jenkins and others, has clearly subverted the boundaries of the missionary axis and is headed into territories hitherto unknown.

I see a burst into new life – greater sense of forgiveness, dependence on prayer, determined participation in and with the community, as well as reinvigorated study of Scripture. There is healing, exorcism, power over witchcraft, and a heightened sense of repentance and growth into likeness of Christ. I notice the hitherto established Anglicans, Methodists, Presbyterians, Catholics, and the Baptists becoming more charismatic. I hear of fasts, overnight vigils, and record attendance at worship services. Indeed the African church is a church that is more renewed, younger, and more charismatic. These are new things; testimonies to a new life in Christ – things that were not part of the identity of the church just about two decades ago. As a theologian, when I see a trend like this, I make an observation: African Christianity is increasingly seeing God not just as a

---

4. G. Kinoti, *Hope for Africa* (Nairobi: AISRED, 1994), 74–75.

5. I need to note here that most theologians are trained in deductive theology. As such they are not used to doing theology from the voices of the situation of reception. For these theologians, the magisterium only has to be implemented in practice. Should the *magisterium* clash with *sensus fidelium*, the former is treated as the norm and the latter is subordinated.

transcendent monad, but as Father who is inviting them into a new life in fellowship with his Son and the Holy Spirit. The great awakenings and conversions the researchers talk about are the work of the Lord, the Holy Spirit, who is also the power over demons, structures and principalities. The Father sends forth the Spirit of power himself. This is our God: Father, Son, Holy Spirit.

## 6.2 The Access: Ubuntu Philosophy

To speak of a God in the Africa nomenclature, one has to make reference to *Ubuntu Philosophy*.[6] This way of interpreting reality was first documented about a half a century ago by Placide Tempels and later improved into its current stature by Griaule and Dieterlen. Renowned ethnophilosophers such as Alexis Kagame, J. Jahn, John S. Mbiti and Cheick A. Diop are all agreed that Tempels, Griaule and Dieterlen made significant contributions to the understanding of the African conceptual framework. Of course, these scholars are not just following Tempels, Griaule and Dieterlen.[7] These scholars have done their own serious research and have, in the face

---

6. Note that this position assumes a fundamental unity as opposed to the much-hyped diversity of Africa. In my book, *The Doctrine of God in African Christian Thought*, I have argued that Africa is culturally and linguistically one. This appears to be the rallying point of the African Renaissance Movement (check what it represents). For in-depth reflection on Ubuntu Philosophy, see, Win van Binsbergen, *Reconciliation*: "A Major African Social Technology of Shared and Recognised Humanity (Ubuntu)," Paper presented at the "Seminar on Culture and Globalization," Human Sciences Research Council, Pretoria; 1999; C. A. Diop, *Precolonial Black Africa* (Brooklyn, New York: Lawrence Hill Books, 1987); M. Fortes and E. E. Evans-Pritchard, *African Political Systems* (London: Oxford University Press, 1940); D. A Masolo, *African Philosophy in Search of Identity* (Bloomington, IN: Indiana University Press, 1994); M. B. Ramose, *African Philosophy through Maim* (Harare: Mond Books, 2002).

7. It should be remembered that the study of African cultures which stressed the metaphysical dimension of the African concept of "being" was not only done by Tempels; others who made significant contributions by 1946 are Griaule (see *Dieu d'Eau: Entretiens avec Ogotommeli* [Paris: Editions du Chêne, 1948], English edition: *Conversations with Ogotommeli* [London: Oxford University Press, 1965]), Dieterlen and Maya Deren. Since the translation of Tempels' book into French in 1945, the book generated more debates than the works of either Griaule or Dieterlen. Consequently, Tempels became the best known of the three. The Tempels' book that we are using here is the 1959 edition of the original book that was published in 1945. It should be noted that these four different authors (Tempels, a Belgian monk, 1945; Griaule, a French ethnographer; Ogotommeli, an African sage, 1946; and Maya Daren, an American author, 1953) came to the conclusion that although the African peoples are different, their conceptual frameworks agree with one another.

of vilification, agreed with Tempels and his company (albeit with modifications).[8]

It is important to note however that Ubuntu Philosophy relates to the African inculturation theology in the same line as the other philosophic traditions already discussed in respect to their respective theologies: Neoplatonism, Aristotelianism, German Idealism and apophatic mysticism. Use of the categories of Ubuntu Philosophy in theology for African is another way of admitting that God in fact tells the African people about himself in simple everyday language. Lamin Sanneh's sentiments below are particularly illuminating:

> People had a right to understand what they were being taught . . . there was nothing God wanted to say which could not be said in a simple everyday language. God would not confound people about the truth, and that made the language of religion compatible with ordinary human understanding. The gospel proclamation stripped religious discourse of the hocus-pocus and elevated the voice of the *volk*.[9]

---

8. Apostel's *African Philosophy* (Gent, Belgium: Story-Scientia, 1981) and Masolo's *African Philosophy in Search of Identity* (Bloomington, IN: Indiana University Press, 1994) explain that Kagame was the first African scholar with solid preparation in philosophy and knowledge of the African ways to give Tempels' hypothesis a better grounding. Besides, they observe, he was also an established scholar of Bantu languages. With this background, Kagame was able to uncover the same concepts that Tempels proposed even though he used a different approach: the analysis of Bantu languages. J. Jahn's book, *Muntu* (New York: Grove Press, 1961), adopts the categories of Kagame and sticks to Tempels' concept of force (p. 99ff.). Mbiti's African *Religions and Philosophy* (London: Heinemann, 1969) sees Tempels' book as having opened "the way for a sympathetic study of African religions and philosophy" (p. 10). Mbiti particularly does not agree with Tempels' idea of "the vital force," but the ontology he proposes (p. 16) resembles that of Tempels and Kagame. Diop does not come out clearly in support of Tempels' cosmology; however, he vigorously argues from the foundations of an African historiography that Africa is and has always been different, and that Africans do not need to be embarrassed by that difference, see his *Precolonial Black Africa* (1987).

9. Lamin Sanneh, *Whose Religion Is Christianity? The Gospel beyond the West* (Grand Rapids, MI: Eerdmans, 2003), 98.

> **Basic Features of Ubuntu Philosophy**
>
> The elements of Ubuntu Philosophy as abstracted from Placide Tempels' *Bantu Philosophy* are as follows:
>
> 1) The existence or the essence of anything is its being a force. To understand what "force" means, one must pay attention to the African people's notion of life and death. The African people view life and death not as absolute concepts but as relative concepts that are to be seen together. Life in this sense is a dynamic process of increase or decrease in "vital force." Under this system of thought, one enjoys a state of well being when his/her life force is strong and is said to be dying when his/her life force is diminishing. Therefore, it is in this sense that Temples can say "force is the nature of being, force is being, being is force."[10]
> 2) Every force is specific, thus different beings are characterized by different intensities and types of forces and yet they are in a relationship of interdependence.[11]
> 3) Each force can either be strengthened or weakened. "One force that is greater than another can paralyze it, diminish it or even cause its operation totally to cease, but for all that, the force does not cease to exist. Existence which comes from God cannot be taken from a creature by any created force."[12]

---

10. P. Tempels, *Bantu Philosophy* (Paris: Présence Africaine, 1969), 49–55.
11. Ibid., 58–61.
12. Ibid., 57.

> 4) The universe is a hierarchy of forces according to their strengths: (1) Above all forces is God – he gives existence to other forces, (2) then come the first fathers and founders of clans – they constitute an important chain binding men to God, (3) then the dead of the tribe, (4) man, (5) animal, (6) vegetable, and (7) mineral.[13] The "chain" explains the absolute necessity of any of these links for balanced existence; thus the saying – "I am because we are." Beings occupying a higher place in the hierarchy can directly influence beings of lower rank.[14]

Alexis Kagame has more carefully explained the chain using NTU root as follows:

> *Umuntu* – this category denotes life forces with intelligence (men, spirits, the living dead). God in this scheme is the *Great Muntu*.
>
> *Ikintu* – this category refers to subordinated powers of things, objects or simply animals, plants and minerals. All these are beings without intelligence.
>
> *Ahantu* – this category describes the power of place and time.
>
> *Ukuntu* – this category suggests the manners (modalities) in which power acts (quality, quantity, relation, action, passion, position and possession).[15]

When we say God within this frame of reference, what is heard immediately is the "great *Muntu*," the "great person," the "great, powerful Life

---

13. Ibid., 63.
14. Ibid., 66–69.
15. See Masolo, *African Philosophy in Search of Identity*, 87; E. G. Parrinder, *Africa's Three Religions* (London: Sheldon Press, 1969), 27; J. S. Mbiti, *African Religions and Philosophy*, 11. Kagame (see Apostel, *African Philosophy*, 70–84) explains that *Umuntu* and *Ikinitu* relates with the Aristotelian category of substance, *Ahantu* with the Aristotelian category of place and time, and *Ukuntu* with the six other Aristotelian categories (quantity, quality, relation, action, passion, position, and possession.).

Force."[16] Elsewhere, Tempels describes God as a "supreme wise man, who knows all things, who established at the deepest level the kind and nature of their forces. He is force itself, which has force within itself, has made all other beings, and knows all forces."[17] Various African peoples know God by such names as *Modimo, Nyame, Nyasaye, Ngai, Mulungu* and so on.[18] A name like *Mulungu*, for example, simply means God. According to D. C. Scott, *Mulungu*[19] does not mean "different forces of nature, not spirits, not

---

16. Tempels, *Bantu Philosophy*, 28.

17. Ibid., 39. Note that Tempels does not say that the Africans understand God as merely a force. Rather, the Africans view God as the "great Muntu," the powerful person and force from which all other things flow. "Muntu" is not merely a force, but it has intelligence and might be described as Mind or a neuter supreme consciousness (see Jahn, *Muntu*, 105; cf. Parrinder, *Africa's Three Religions*, 27f.). Works of scholars such as P. M. Steyne, *Gods of Power: A Study of Beliefs and Practices of Animists* (Houston, TX: Touch Publications, 1989), which come from the commitment to animism and proceed to require the African sense of God to fit into their mould (see p. 40–41) are, therefore, way off-line.

18. Christoph Barth argues that the name *Yahweh* did not drop from heaven, "it was God himself who came down. Revealing himself to Israel he adopted Israel's language. His name is rooted in this language. It is taken from words and names in the daily speech of the Hebrews." C. Barth, *God with Us: A Theological Introduction to the Old Testament*, ed. G. W. Bromiley (Grand Rapids, MI: Eerdmans, 1991), 71. Moreover, the fathers of Israel had no problem whatsoever in invoking *Yahweh* by divine names that originated in the religious life of the neighboring Gentiles. See also the argument of E. W. Smith: "Christian missionaries in their teachings and translations of Scripture have adopted African names of God. This practice has been criticized on the ground that pagan terms can never express Christian truth. There is a pragmatic sanction for what they do. The Hebrew *elohim* was a class name covering many supernatural beings. . . . When the Hebrew Scripture was translated into Greek, *elohim* was rendered *theos* and the sacred personal name Yahwe kurios, 'Lord.' Greek-speaking Christians as well as Jews of the Diaspora accepted these as equivalents. . . . Teutonic peoples had their own god-names – Wodan, god of the dead, Donar, god of thunder and the sky, Tyr, god of war. The Christian missionaries took over not these personal names, but the class word god, which denoted (according to the Oxford Dictionary) a superhuman person who was worshiped as having power over nature and the fortunes of mankind; and also an image or other object which was worshiped. Whatever it meant to our Teutonic forefathers it did not mean what it means to us today: Christianity took it and filled it with new content. Christian missionaries in Africa differ from their predecessors in Europe for they have generally not adopted class names like *theos* or *god* but personal names like Nyame, Leza, Nyambe." E. W. Smith, *African Ideas of God* (London: Edinburgh House Press, 1950), 34–35.

19. See logic for "Yahweisation" of African names for God. C. E. L. Heureux, *Rank among the Canaanite Gods: El, Baal, and the Rephaim* (Ann Arbor, MI: Scholars Press, 1979); cf. D. J Bosch, "God in Africa; Implications for Kerygma," *Missionalia* 1, no. 1 (1973): 12–17. David Bosch argues that from the beginning Yahweh was not completely identical with El. El appeared as Yahweh and yet there was a degree of discontinuity; however, in spite of this, Yahweh took over the names of El and his functions. El, according to David Bosch, J. Blommendaal, Albrecht Alt, B. Gemser, Rolf Rendtorff, Otto Eissfeldt, Georg Fohrer, F. M. Cross and M. J. Mulder, was the gate through which Yahweh penetrated the Semitic

fetish, but God, the Creator, Spirit, Almighty, Personal God. . . . you can't put the plural with God because God is one."[20] This God is also spoken of as mystery God experienced with a sense of numinousness otherwise described by G. M. Satiloane as the *mysterium tremendum* and the *fascinans*.[21]

## 6.3 The Trinitarian Moment

The movement from the African idea of God in Category 1 above to the biblical depiction is to say the least revolutionary – a sudden turning point. It is a conversion experience[22] in which the African world re-orients and reconfigures the God it has known by such personal names as *Modimo*, *Nyame*, *Nyasaye*, *Ngai*, *Mulungu* in biblical terms: Father, Son and Holy Spirit. The experience here is a refocusing of the African pre-Christian idea of God and all its cultural/social underpinnings in the light of the God now known in Jesus Christ. In other words, *Modimo*, *Nyame*, *Nyasaye*, *Ngai*, and *Mulungu* known in Christ becomes the sole inhabitant of the Divine category of our pre-Christian cosmology.

This new understanding of God among the African Christians not only runs against the notion that the African peoples were *tabula rasa* as far as knowledge of God is concerned, but on a more fundamental note, it stands to confirm that the African primal world in fact talked of God as one referent reality. The African convert can now confirm, as Karl Rahner suggests,

> knowledge of the unique, transcendent, personal God which
> is always stirring into life, whether naturally or supernaturally

---

world. According to Bosch, the "Gods of Africa" are like El. They must allow themselves to be taken over by Yahweh or else they are Baal (Bosch, "God in Africa," 15–17).

20. D. C. Scott, *Dictionary of the Nyanja Language*, ed. A. Heatherwick (London: Religious Tract Society, 1929), 348.

21. See G. M. Setiloane, "Modimo: God among the Sotho-Tswana," *Journal of Theology for Southern Africa* 4, no. 4 (September 1973) 6–7; cf. his *The Image of God among the Sotho-Tswana* (Rotterdam : Balkema, 1976), 78f.; G. M. Setiloane, *African Theology: An Introduction* (Johannesburg: Skotaville Publishers, 1986), 33.

22. See Sanneh's definition of conversion: "A re-orientation of the worldview so that the old moral framework was reconfigured without being overthrown. It was not that the old spells, turning benign from overuse, had dulled the appetite, but that, under challenge, their spent potency sparked a clamor for a valiant God. People sensed in their hearts that Jesus did not mock their respect for the sacred or their clamor for an invincible Savior, so they beat their sacred drums for him until the stars skipped and danced in the skies. After that the stars weren't little anymore" (Sanneh, *Whose Religion Is Christianity?*, 43).

> . . . Second, the Christian conception will always express God's passionate protest against every kind of polytheistic or pantheistic deification of the world . . . Third, it alone will be able to say unambiguously and definitively just how the personal, transcendent desires *in actual fact* to stand to the world in his sovereign freedom: namely, as the God who actually discloses his inmost self to man out of grace . . . As the God who gives his definitive sanction to the world in the incarnation of his Son and summons it to share in his Triune life.[23]"

In other words, the encounter of the African world with Christianity kicks off a process in which *Modimo, Nyame, Nyasaye, Ngai,* and *Mulungu* are at once a mystery – the One is the Three and the One at the same time, moreover his absolute transcendence is also overcome. *Nyasaye* now exists in the balance between transcendence and immanence. This *Nyasaye* now bursts the boundaries of known cosmology and a new language to express this new existential reality bursts forth. In the case of independencies and the charismatic groups, the new language is often found in songs, colors and signs. The Divine category, which was formerly a monad, is now split into three; yet not three gods, but one God thrice named as *Nyasaye Wuoro* (God the Father), God the Son (*Nyasaye Wuowi*), God the Holy Spirit (*Nyasaye Roho Maler*) and existing in a *perichoresis*. John the Damascene, on the *perichoresis* nature of the existence of the Three, writes:

> The subsistences dwell and are established firmly in one another. For they are inseparable and cannot part from one another, but keep to their separate courses within one another, without coalescing or mingling, but cleaving to each other. For the Son is in the Father and the Spirit: and the Spirit in the Father and the Son: and the Father in the Son and the Spirit, but there is no coalescence or commingling or confusion. And there is one and the same motion: for there is one

---

23. Rahner, *Theological Investigations* I, 85–86.

impulse and one motion of the three subsistences, which is not to be observed in any created nature.[24]

The idea of the Divine *perichoresis* is nuanced. Athanasius, for instance, understood it as coinherence: the Father in the Son and the Son in the Father. In other words "a complete mutual indwelling in which each Person, while remaining what he is by himself as Father, Son or Holy Spirit, is wholly in others as the others are wholly in him."[25] Gregory of Nyssa approached the issue from the conception that the divine Persons mutually "contain one another." For Gregory of Nyssa, the Father and the Son are receptive and permeative (*choretikos*) of one another. The idea "containing one another" is understood in the sense of the mutual envelopment of one another.[26] According to Gregory Nazianzen, Wuoro (the Father), Wuowi (the Son) and Roho Maler (the Holy Spirit) are "entirely one with those with whom he is conjoined, as he is in himself, because of the identity of being and power that is between them. This is the reason for the Oneness so far as we have apprehended it. If this reason has force, thanks be to God for the insight; if it is not, let us seek a stronger one."[27]

The doctrine of *perichoresis* in a way resonates with the African notion of person and has significant ethical dimension: "I am because we are." However its true significance lies in modeling how we are to exist with God, with fellow human beings and with the rest of God's creation. The church Fathers contemplated the idea of "person" as existence in the way God exists. Thus for them, the image of God in man had to do with how to exist in the way God exists. Man, according to this point of view, is free to "affect the how of his existence either in the direction of the way (the

---

24. Church Fathers: *An Exposition of the Orthodox Faith* Book I, (John Damascus), Chapter 14. *Properties of the Divine Nature.* See http://www.newadvent.org/fathers/33041.htm accessed on 18 June 2009.

25. Torrance, *The Trinitarian Perspective,* 10.

26. Gregory, Bishop of Nyssa, "Against Sabellius," in *Nicene and Post-Nicene Fathers of the Christian Church,* vol. IX, ed. P. Schaff (Grand Rapids, MI: Eerdmans, 1891). See *adv. et Sab*.12; 266.

27. Athanasius, Hilary, Gregory of Nyssa and Gregory of Nazianzen all understood *homoousios* as conveying the concept of the co-inherence of the three persons in the one identical being of God. However, patristic theology owes the term *perichoretic relation* to Gregory of Nazianzen, who applied it to the way in which the Divine exists. (See Gregory Nazianzen, "Oratio." Relevant sections are *Oratio*. 31.16, see also 31.14; cf. 25.16, 26.19, and 42.15ff. 18.42).

*how*) God is, or in the direction of *what* his, i.e. man's nature is." Man can live either according to the human nature or in the way God exists – that is, in the image of God's personhood.[28] For the church Fathers therefore, "person" is the how or the way of being of God himself. God does not exist in isolation; he exists in a communion. The Father exists in love and relationship with the Son and the Holy Spirit. Yet in this relationship there is also the question of the personal identity that should not be lost to view. Father, Son and the Holy Spirit are hypostases thus they indicate personal identity in the divine interrelationship but they also provide how they exist, thus a pattern to which we must pay attention.

The diagram below then is an attempt at an explanation of what would be going on in my mind as an African Christian when I say God. I am immediately reminded of *Nyasaye* (God) and how he relates to the entire African cosmology (see categories 1–6), and then to Nyasaye's internal relationships (category 1).

| **Category 1**<br>NYASAYE (GOD) = the only one with the "divine force" – NTU.<br>The ultimate explanation of the origin<br>and sustenance of both man and all things. |
|---|
| **Category 2**<br>SPIRITS = every spirit distinguished by the nature of its "force" – NTU.<br>Some spirits are weaker than the others. |
| **Category 3**<br>ANCESTORS = superhuman beings and the spirits of men who died a long time ago but still active in determining the affairs of the living.<br>Each of the ancestors distinguished by their respective "life force" – NTU. |

---

28. J. D. Zizioulas, "The Doctrine of the Holy Trinity: The Significance of the Cappadocian Contribution," in *Trinitarian Theology Today*, ed. C. Schwöbel (Edinburgh: T. & T. Clark, 1995), 55.

| **Category 4** |
|---|
| MAN = Human beings who are alive and who are about to be born. Each human being distinguished by respective "life force" – NTU. |

| **Category 5** |
|---|
| ANIMALS & PLANTS = Or remainder of biological life. Each of these distinguished by respective "life force" – NTU. |

| **Category 6** |
|---|
| PHENOMENA & OBJECTS WITHOUT BIOLOGICAL LIFE = rocks, space, time, beauty. Each is distinguished by respective force. |

*Nyasaye's* internal relationship (description of category 1) must factor in the One who exists in the Three who are "inseparable and cannot part," the three columns indicate the three keeping their "separate courses within one another, without coalescing or mingling, but cleaving to each other."[29]

| God the Son (*Wuowi*) = "the only-begotten Son of God, begotten of the Father before all worlds; God of God, Light of Light, very God of very God; begotten, not made, . . . one . . . with the Father, by whom all things were made." | God the Father (*Wuoro*) = "maker of heaven and earth, and all things visible and invisible." | God the Holy Spirit (*Roho Maler*) = "the Lord and Giver of Life; who proceeds from the Father and the Son; who with the Father and the Son together is worshiped and glorified; who spoke by the prophets." |
|---|---|---|

The personal identity of the hypostases is sorted for me by the relationships: the Father as *monarchia*, the Son is begotten of the Father and the Holy Spirit proceeds from the Father and rests in the Son. The Father eternally begets the Son. In other words, time does not come into play in this relationship. He existed from the eternal past with the Father. Thus we can

---

29. Church Fathers, *An Exposition of the Orthodox Faith*, Chapter 14.

say with Hilary of Poitiers that the Son is a perfect offspring of the Father and that as opposed to creation, he is endowed with the properties that are in the Father. Elsewhere Hilary argues that the Son is derived wholly from the whole of his Father's nature (NTU), in other words, he has the whole of his Father's nature (NTU), and thus he both abides in and belongs in the same category as the Father.[30] The Spirit proceeds from the Father but "rests" in the Son.[31] The procession is of eternal nature; in other words the Spirit proceeds from the Father from the eternal past. Similarly, the Spirit has the whole of the Father's nature thus he too belongs in the Father's category. The Three are then distinguished thus:

> For the Father is without cause and unborn: for He is derived from nothing, but derives from Himself His being, nor does He derive a single quality from another. Rather He is Himself the beginning and cause of the existence of all things in a definite and natural manner. But the Son is derived from the Father after the manner of generation, and the Holy Spirit likewise is derived from the Father, yet not after the manner of generation, but after that of procession. And we have learned that there is a difference between generation and procession, but the nature of that difference we in no wise understand. Further, the generation of the Son from the Father and the procession of the Holy Spirit are simultaneous.[32]

## 6.4 The Father: The Divine *Monarchia*

The Fatherhood of God is known in Africa. John S. Mbiti for instance notes that pre-Christian Africa viewed God as the universal creator-father.[33] He is referred to as excavator, hewer, carver, creator, originator, inventor, architect, potter, fashioner by different African peoples in their description

---

30. Hilary, Bishop of Poitiers, "*De Trinitate*," in *Nicene and Post-Nicene Fathers of the Christian Church*, vol. IX, ed. P. Schaff (Grand Rapids, MI: Eerdmans, 1891). See 3.1; 2, 4. See also Church Fathers, *An Exposition of the Orthodox Faith*, chapter 8.

31. Church Fathers, *An Exposition of the Orthodox Faith*, chapter 8.

32. Ibid.

33. Mbiti, *African Religions and Philosophy*, 39.

of God. Indeed he is referred to as one who fathered the world, owns it and cares for it. He is the unfathered Father and therefore self-existent.[34] This pre-Christian view of God (*Nyasaye*) is going through a major re-orientation in light of the Christian faith.

*Nyasaye* is indeed the creator-father but more than anything else the Christian content brings in something else: he is the unoriginated origin of the *Wuowi* (the Son) and of the *Roho Maler* (Holy Spirit). Now he exists, not alone but in an eternal *perichoresis* with the *Wuowi* and *Roho Maler*. With the church fathers and John the Damascene, the African Christians can confess:

> (We believe) in one Father, the beginning, and cause of all: begotten of no one: without cause or generation, alone subsisting: creator of all: but Father of one only by nature, His Only-begotten Son and our Lord and God and Savior Jesus Christ, and Producer of the most Holy Spirit.[35]

The divine category, formerly a monad in the previous intellectual culture, is now split into three (a triad); but the Father, who is the unoriginated origin of the Son and the Holy Spirit is the One. The African nomenclature suggests that a father cannot be a brother to his son. St Basil sustains the same argument in his statement of *homoousios*. He says that the Father and Son are not *homoousios* in the sense of being "brothers." However "when both the cause and that which has its origin from that cause are of the same nature, then they are called *homoousios*." However, unlike the case of coins which are *homoousios* to each other and are therefore "brothers," the Son is *homoousios* to the Father because all that he has he receives from the Father.[36] This is also the case in the African logic that a father cannot be a brother to his son. The Father is the "source" of his son. Note that fatherhood here is not primarily linked to "authority"; rather it is linked to "source." Father however is often understood as "source" not in the static

---

34. J. S. Mbiti, *Introduction to African Religion* (London: Heinemann, 1975), 44.

35. Church Fathers, *An Exposition of the Orthodox Faith*, chapter 8.

36. St Basil of Caesarea, "St. Basil: Letters and Select Works," in vol. 8 of *A Select Library of Nicene and Post-Nicene Fathers of the Christian Church*, eds. Philip Schaff and Henry Wace (New York: The Christian Literature Company, 1890–1900), Epistle 52.

sense, but in the sense that he also "engages" the Son and the Son on the other hand reveals the Father.

Going back to St Basil's presentation, we find a pattern which helps us to put into proper perspective the *monarchia* of the *Nyasaye* without subordinating the *Wuowi* (the Son) and the *Roho Maler* (the Holy Spirit). Note that St Basil the Great talks of *homousion* but without talking of a divine *ousia* underlying the hypostases. Instead he talks of *Nyasaye*'s *ousia* which he shares with the Son by begetting him and with the Holy Spirit by procession. John Calvin ends up with the same argument but instead of comtemplating *ousia* from the perspective of *monarchia* he prefers *principium divinitatis*.[37] Using Tempels' logic, *Nyasaye* shares with the *Wuowi* (the Son) his "divine life-force" – UTU by generation and the *Roho Maler* (the Holy Spirit) does the same by procession. They are therefore coequal in this sense.

## 6.5 The Holy Spirit

The term Holy Spirit presented the first translators of the Bible into the African languages with a special difficulty because they needed to separate the Holy Spirit from God on the one hand and from the spirits on the other hand. There are African words for "Holy" and "Spirit" but, as Mbiti explains, "the combination which gives us the 'Holy Spirit' as part of the Trinity is specifically Christian heritage."[38] In the context of the Bantus of East African, for instance, the Kiswahili word "*Roho*" was adopted to represent the concept of the Holy Spirit instead of the vernacular words for

---

37. Calvin prefers to use the term, *pricipium divinitatis*. By this term he meant that Christ is not from himself; he has a beginning in the Father. He is quick to add, however, that the *prinicipium divinitas* has to do with order and position and not ontological priority (J. Calvin, *Institutes of the Christian Religion*, trans. E. L. Battles [London: Collins, 1986], I:13.6, 18, 20–25). For Calvin the Father is not merely the "Divine *arche*" that we see in the Cappadocians, for Deity can never be derived. Christ is Divine – both because of the *homoousios* and because he is the Son. One being of God is wholly common to the Father and the Son (Ibid., I:13.2, 7f., 23) and, on the other hand, "unless the Father were God, he could not be the Father, and unless the Son were God, he could not be the Son" thus Christ's being is without *principium* except that of the Father (Ibid., I:13.25).

38. J. S. Mbiti, "The Holy Spirit in African Independent Churches," in *Festschrift Günther Wagner*, ed. Günter Wagner (New York: Peter Lang, 1994), 103.

spirit.[39] The Protestant Acholi of Uganda adopted *Cwiny Maleng* (heart) while their Catholic counterparts adopted *Tipu Maleng* (shadow, depiction and ancestral spirit) and *Maleng* that specifically refer to either physical or ethical purity.[40] Although (from these two examples) the new concept *Roho* and *Cwiny Maleng* or *Tipu Maleng* refer to the third person of the Trinity, the exact reference of the theological terms *Roho, Cwiny Maleng* or *Tipu Maleng* has remained elusive to many African Christians due to the traditional interferences imposed by cosmological structures.

| Son = "by whom all things were made," . . . "for us men and for our salvation," . . . sits on the right hand of the Father; and He shall come again, with glory, to judge the quick and the dead; whose kingdom shall have no end. | Father = "maker of heaven and earth, and all things visible and invisible." | Holy Spirit = "the Lord and Giver of Life; who proceeds from the Father and the Son; who with the Father and the Son together is worshiped and glorified; who spoke by the prophets.' |
|---|---|---|
| Spirits, divinities ||| 
| Ancestors, heroes |||
| Human beings=men, women |||
| Animals and plants |||
| Phenomenon and objects without biological life (space, time, beauty, pain, structures, etc.) |||

---

39. J. N. K. Mugambi, *The African Heritage and Contemporary Christianity* (Nairobi: Longman Kenya, 1989), 65.

40. H. Behrend, *Alice Lakwena and the Holy Spirits: War in Northern Uganda 1985-97* (Nairobi: EAEP, 1999), 116.

The Spirit is a hypostasis of God who applies the Son to our world. In this respect therefore, I see African Christianity conceptualizing the Holy Spirit as shown in the figure on the previous page.

Whereas the Spirit receives equal adoration and glorification with the Father and Son, he applies Christ and his benefits until he returns (*ordo salutis*) to all categories of the African cosmology as the one who is fountain of life and wholeness, creative, all-effecting, all-ruling, all-powerful, Lord of all creation, filling, shared in, sanctifying, the intercessor, receiving the supplications of all, participated in by all creation, though himself creating, and investing with life, and maintaining the universe.[41] The church fathers appear to have had this in mind when they said the Spirit "gives also to all things being according to their several natures, and it is itself the being of existing things, the life of living things, the reason of rational beings, the thought of thinking beings. But it is itself above mind and reason and life and essence."[42]

The Holy Spirit does this as the "breath of life" – "the principle of life" (see Gen 2:7; Job 33:4). He is the only hypostasis from which life flows. The Holy Spirit applies Christ to all the categories: "spirits and divinities"; "ancestors and heroes"; "human beings"; "animals and plants"; and "phenomenon and objects without biological life and greater areas of life such as political activity and consummation of new age."[43] Consequently, the entire cosmology receives the benefit of Christ (Eph 1:3; cf. 1 Cor 1:5, 30) immediately, simultaneously, and eschatologically due to the work of the *Roho Maler* (Holy Spirit).

## 6.6 The Son

The Son in his independent hypostasis is differentiated from the Father from whom he proceeds; however he displays in himself the same attributes

---

41. Compare this to John the Damascene's position as recorded in Church Fathers, *An Exposition of the Orthodox Faith*, chapter 8.

42. Church Fathers, *An Exposition of the Orthodox Faith*, chapter 14.

43. For relevant scriptural references. Jer 31:31ff. talks of a situation that has arisen as a result of God's direct work. The same theme is carried in Isa 11:9. Other references discussing more or less the same theme are Zech 12:10; Joel 2: 18ff.; 3:1f. The others are Isa 11:2; 42:1, cf. 61:1; 32:15; 44:3; Ezek 39:29; 11:19; 36:26f.

of the Father. In the Nicene Creed the phrase "being of one substance with the Father" is literally translated as "one with the Father – *en achiel chutho gi Wuoro.*" This reads very much like the pre-Nicene language. His coming and reign is related vitally to the sending and the authority of the Father. In other words, there is no Christ apart from the One who sent him. The Bible appears to depict the ministry of Christ in all its array as related to the one who sent him; the Father.

This reorientation is likely to challenge the Christologies from below as a dominant reflective pattern in African theology. The fact that he declares the Father as the one who is *homoousios* with him simply implies that in this case Christology from above is most adequate. But on a more significant note, it is an absolute affirmation to the regenerated/doxological African church for whom the Son's work has been accomplished (*historia salutis*). John S. Mbiti explains what he perceives to be the reason Africans in their masses have taken seriously the relevance of Christ:

> It is highly doubtful that even at their very best, those other religious systems and ideologies current in Africa are saying anything radically new to, and different from what is already embedded in Christianity. And yet the strength and uniqueness of Christianity do not lie in the fact that its teaching, practice and history have all the major elements of the other religious traditions. The uniqueness of Christianity is in Jesus Christ. . . . it is He, therefore, and only He, who deserves to be the goal and standard for individuals and mankind.[44]

Whereas Mbiti in the above excerpt has talked only in generalities, I wish to state two specific factors that I see as having contributed to Africa's phenomenal attraction to Christ: (1) The immanence of God accomplished by the Son and (2) the view of relationship with Christ as directly linked to the life-death continuum.

## Solution to Transcendence-Immanence Question

In the pre-Christian cosmology, God is very transcendent. The mediation of God to man is through the spirits and the divinities. Notice in the

---

44. Mbiti, *African Religions and Philosophy*, 277.

figure on page 117 that between the "human beings" and the "spirits and divinities" lies another whole category of existence thereby rendering the Divine even more transcendent. The Zulu informants of Bishop Callaway admitted to him in apparent frustration that the *izibongo* (praise names) of Nkulukulu were no longer known.[45]

> The oldmen say that *uNkulukulu* is *umVelingqangi*, for they say he came out first; they say he is the *uhlanga* from which all men broke off. The oldmen say that *uNkulukulu* is; he made the first men, and ancients of long ago; the ancients of long ago died; there remained those who had been begotten by them, sons, by whom we hear that there were ancients of long ago who knew the breaking off of the world. They did not know *uNkulukulu*; they did not see him with their eyes; they heard it said that *uNkulukulu* was. He came out where men broke off from *uhlanga*. He begat the ancients of long ago. They died and left their children. They begat others, their sons, they died. They begat others; thus we at length have heard about *uNkulukulu*. It was our ancestors who told us the accounts of *uNkulukulu* and of the ancients of long ago. Tell me if at the present time there are any who pray to *uNkulukulu*? There are none. They pray to the *amatongo* (men who have died).[46]

Although the traditional Zulus recognize the transcendence of uNkulukulu, they view it as a disturbing reality and they look forward to a time when uNkulukulu will emerge and in a sense be immanent.

> This then is what I maintain, if anyone says he understands all about *uNkulukulu*. I say all men would be glad to go to the man who says this to see him and to hear him; for in process of time we have come to worship the *amadhlozi* only, because we knew not what to say about *uNkulukulu*; for we do not even know where we separated from him, nor the word which

---

45. Smith, *African Ideas of God*, 106.

46. H. Callaway, *The Religious System of the Amazulu* (London: Routledge and Kagan Paul, 1870), 13.

he left with us. It is on that account then that we seek out for ourselves the *amadhlozi* that we not always be thinking about *uNkulukulu*, saying: "*uNkulukulu* has left us", or "What has he done for us?"[47]

The Lango of Uganda are similar to the Zulu in this regard. The Lango admit that they know nothing of Gabipiny (God – literally the one who sees the universe). This is because Gabipiny is watching the universe, but from a distance. The Venda do not say much about Mwali except that he is the highest in the hierarchy of beings and therefore stay very far.[48] The Dinka solve the problem of the transcendence of God by pointing to the mystery of life. A Dinka will say: I do not know the fine details about Nhialic (Dinka word for God), but because I have life, I know Nhialic exists.

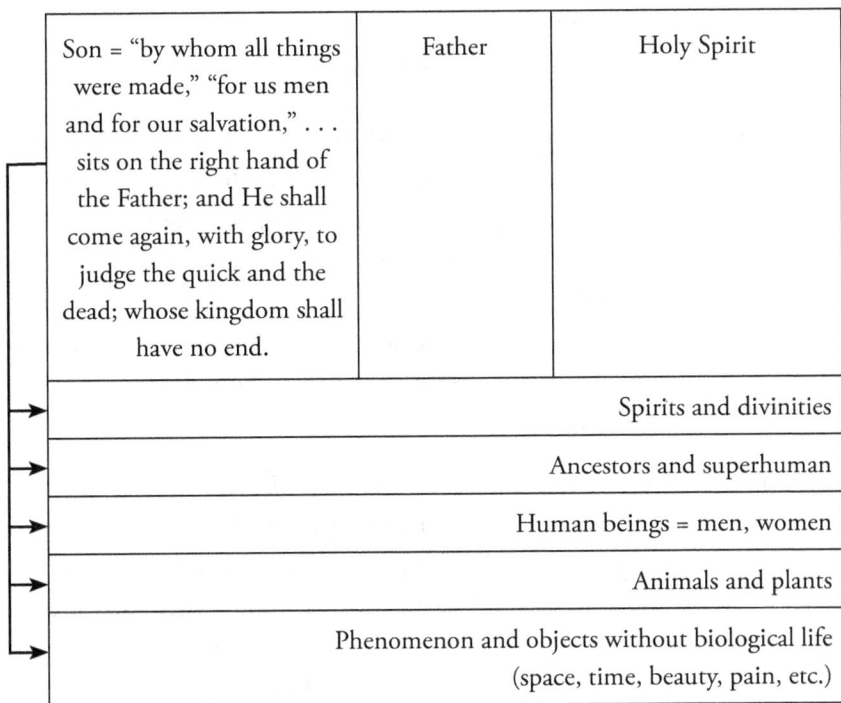

---

47. Ibid., 31.
48. J. A. van Rooy, *The Traditional World View of the Black People in Southern Africa* (Potchefstroom: Instituut vir die Bevordering van Calvinisme, 1978), 5.

For me, the mediatorship of Christ has tremendous implication for the transcendence of God. Divinities, spirits and ancestors derive their significance from the transcendence of God, which as we have seen is a universal problem in African cosmology. The diagram above is an attempt to capture the African Christian's construction of access to God. Now the Christian does not need to go through the spirits, divinities, ancestors or the heroes of the community. Christ became one of us – a human being – and ascended to the very Father who sent him. Unlike the disembodied spirits, and divinities who have no idea what it means to be in this body, Christ in his resurrected body is pleading on our behalf with the Father who sent him and from whom he generates and with whom he exists in a *perichoretic* relationship. Christ in keeping with his ministry opens the line between humankind and God, but even in this activity we do not share God's unique category and therefore become "gods." Put differently, God has come down to us without us becoming "gods."[49]

The Son as the sent one of God has the key to all the categories of the African reality as the arrows show in away that confirms the personal and the spiritual nature of God's dealings with creation while at the same time safeguarding God's majesty. As a result of the Son's mitigation, humankind is able to access God through him without the requirement for intermediaries (spirits, divinities, ancestors, heroes of tribes). But the arrows from the Son also indicate that he is the one who locks and opens each of the categories. Whatever keys any of the categories may have either for itself or for another category is given by delegation from the Son. As such he is Lord over all, he is the only sent one.

## Relationship with the Son as a Matter of Life and Death

To understand this point, one must put together the Son as co-creator with Africa's concept of the idea of life-death. Tempels has explained that "vital force" is linked to life and death. In this context therefore, life and death are not viewed as absolute concepts; rather they are relative concepts that are to be seen together. Life is seen as a dynamic process of increase or decrease in "vital force." One is said to be in a state of full life when his or her life force is on the upward side and is said to be dying when his or

---

49. Church Fathers, *An Exposition of the Orthodox Faith*, chapter 8.

her life is evidently diminishing. In this sense "vital force" can simply be synonymous with life, provided life is understood to be capable of existing in a continuum where at one end it is 100 percent, whereas at the other, for instance where life has ceased, it is 0 percent.[50] Note that where this life-death continuum holds there is also the view that every force is specific, for instance, one can talk of cats' force, pigs' force, apples' force and so on. Thus different beings are characterized by different intensities and types of forces and yet they are in a relationship of interdependence.[51] Each force can either be strengthened or weakened. In the Tempels' own words: "One force that is greater than another can paralyse it, diminish it or even cause its operation totally to cease, but for all that the force does not cease to exist." Finally, that life comes only from God. Once life is given, other forces can only paralyse it but it is only God who can take it away.[52]

There are so many things in the African world that indicate a diminished life force for most of the known categories. Disease, poverty, environmental challenges, cross-border conflicts, starvation, and so on. Africa yearns for new life – for eradication of diseases, poverty alleviation, working state machineries, restored environment, and so on. In Kenya, for instance, it is common to hear of national prayer days in the event of especially trying moments. In such events, the top leader of the country and his entire battery often participates. The national admission in this case is simply that "our force" (life) is diminished as individuals and as a nation. In other words, we are "dying" unless God "increases the life force" to a bearable level; in other words unless by his direct mitigation God injects new life.

The relevance of the Son in all this is that he has accomplished and finished the plan of salvation of the world and purchased our redemption. Nothing escapes the *historia salutis* of the Son. The Son is a gift to us in his incarnation, crucifixion, death, resurrection and ascension (Phil 2:12, 13; 2 Cor 3:6ff.; Gal 2:20; Col 31–34). His work is therefore sufficient and will never have to be done again for both creation and redemption the two of which being looked at as "the valid permanent order and the new act of

---

50. Tempels, *Bantu Philosophy*, 49–55.
51. Ibid., 58–61.
52. Ibid., 57.

God, the static and the dynamic, the present and the future."[53] However he is presently a prophet, priest and king on account of the finished work and so he is still ruling his people, interceding on their behalf as well as making known his word to his people. For the African cosmology this means: (1) the Son is not sharing his authority with the spirits and the divinities; he must take away the keys from them; (2) the Son is to introduce his agents (biblical angelology) into this category; (3) the Son is to create "the land of the dead" as seventh category below "objects without life" where the dead are locked and are not in contact with other categories until the Second Coming; and finally (4) new life in Christ is to be nurtured in the context of questions raised by the cosmology.

## 6.7 Conclusion

It is difficult to be exhaustive in a work like this. But at least the following are noteworthy: (1) the three hypostases form the beginning point and they are united in a perichoretic relationship; (2) the hypostasis of the Father is the *ousia*; and (3) the *Ubuntu* philosophy, which by its very nature uses some form of apophatic mysticism, provides the categories of speech and the conceptual framework within which the discourse is carried.

The presentation here is the doctrine of the Trinity that emerges from the worship and the personal coming of God in the Son and the Holy Spirit. This for me is a confirmation that the Trinity first and foremost is not an adjunct in theology and neither is it a mere doctrine of abstraction but to the contrary, it is a salvific reality experienced in Jesus Christ and the Holy Spirit.

Trinitarian discussions have historically happened as talks between the two centers – the West and the East. By this, both the West and the East assumed ownership of alternative *magisterium*. This chapter in a sense also functions as an assessment of the extent to which theology takes seriously *sensus fidelium* on the one hand and the *magisterium* on the other. We need an honest assessment of all this not because we want recognition of other global theological communities, important as this may be, but because we are an authentic living Christian community seeking to be obedient to God

---

53. Eichrodt, *Theology of the Old Testament*, 80.

whose coming in Jesus Christ has enjoined us one to another. Christianity has more centers than two. This chapter is a testimony to the richness of the wider Christian world and how much the faith stands to gain by hearing all the voices, especially the emerging voices.

# Bibliography

Adeyemo, T. "The Salvation Debate and Evangelical Response." *East African Journal of Evangelical Theology* 2 (1984): 4–19.

———. *Salvation in an African Tradition*. Nairobi: Evangel Publishing House, 1979.

Apostel, L. *African Philosophy*. Gent, Belgium: Story-Scientia, 1981.

Aquinas, *On Being and Essence*. Translated and annotated by J. J. O'Meara. New York: Newman, 1961.

———. *On the Truth of the Catholic Faith*. Translated by A. C. Pegis, J. F. Anderson and V. F. Bourke. Notre Dame, IN: University of Notre Dame Press, 1975.

———. *Summa Contra Gentiles*. Translated by A. C. Pegis, J. F. Anderson and V. F. Bourke. Notre Dame, IN: University of Notre Dame Press, 1956.

———. *Summa Theologica*. 3 Volumes. Translated by Fathers of English Dominican Province. New York: Benzinger Brothers, inc., 1947.

Aristotle. *De Anima*. New York: Arno Press, 1976.

———. *Metaphysics*. London: Dent, 1956.

Augustine Bishop of Hippo. "Confessions Book 2." In *Nicene and Post Nicene Fathers of the Christian Church*, vol. I, edited by P. Schaff. Grand Rapids: Eerdmans, 1994.

———. "De Trinitate." In *Basic Writings of St Augustine*, vol. II, edited by E. J. Oates. New York: Random House, 1948.

Barth, C. *God with Us: A Theological Introduction to the Old Testament*. Edited by G. W. Bromiley, Grand Rapids, MI: Eerdmans, 1991.

Barth, K. *Church Dogmatics I: The Doctrine of the Word of God, Part 1*. Edinburgh: T. & T. Clark, 1955.

———. *Church Dogmatics I: The Doctrine of the Word of God, Part 2*. Edinburgh: T. & T. Clark, 1956.

———. *Church Dogmatics II: The Doctrine of God Part 1, The Knowledge of God*. Edinburgh: T. & T. Clark, 1957.

———. *Fides Quarens Intellectum. Anselm's Proof of the Existence of God in the Context of His Theological Scheme*. Translated by Ian W. Robertson. London: SCM Press, 1960.

Battaglia, V. "An Examination of Karl Rahner's Trinitarian Theology." *Australian E-Journal of Theology* 9, no. 1 (March 2007): 1–18.

Bediako, K. *Theology and Identity*. Oxford: Regnum Books, 1992.

Behrend, H. *Alice Lakwena and the Holy Spirits: War in Northern Uganda 1985-97*. Nairobi: EAEP, 1999.

Berkhof, H. *Introduction to the Study of Dogmatics*. Translated by J. Vriend. Grand Rapids, MI: Eerdmans, 1985.

Boethius, A. M. S. *The Theological Tractates and the Consolation of Philosophy*. Revised and Translated by H. F. Stewart and E. K. Rand. London: William Heinemann, 1918.

Boff, L. *Trinity and Society*. Maryknoll, NY: Orbis Books, 1988.

Bosch, D. J. "God in Africa; Implications for Kerygma." *Missionalia* 1, no. 1 (1973): 3–21.

Braaten, C. E. *Our Naming of God: Problems and Prospects of God-Talk Today*. Minneapolis, MN: Fortress Press, 1981.

Broadbent, E. H. *The Pilgrim Church*. London: Pickering & Inglis Ltd., 1931.

Bruce, F. F. *The Spreading Flame*. Exeter, England: The Paternoster Press, 1958.

Bulgakov, S. *The Comforter*. Translated by Boris Jakim. Grand Rapids: Eerdmans, 2004.

———. *Sophia: The Wisdom of God*. Translated by the Rev. Patrick Thompson, the Rev. O. Fielding Clarke and Miss Xenia Braikevitc, Hudson: Lindisfarne Press, 1993. Revised edition of *The Wisdom of God: A Brief Summary of Sophiology*. New York: The Paisley Press, 1937.

———. *Svet neverchernii* [*The Unfading Light*]. Moscow: Izdatel'stvo 'Respublika,' 1994.

Butler, D. J. *Four Philosophies and Their Use in Education and Religion*. New York: Harper and Brothers Publishers, 1950.

Byaruhanga-Akiiki, A. "African Traditional Values for Human Development." In *Church Contributions to Integral Development*, edited by Deogratias M. Byabazaire, Joseph Thérèse Agbasiere, and Boniface K. Zabajungu, 45–62. Eldoret: Gaba Publications, 1989.

———. "Spirituality in African Traditions." BOLESWA Occasional Papers on Theology and Religion. Number 1. University of Botswana, Lesotho and Swaziland, 1988.

Calvin, J. *Institutes of the Christian Religion*. Translated by E. L. Battles. London: Collins, 1986.

Callaway, H. *The Religious System of the Amazulu*. London: Routledge and Kagan Paul, 1870.

# Bibliography

Charlesworth, J. H., ed. *The Messiah: Developments in Earliest Judaism and Christianity.* Minneapolis: Fortress Press, 1992.

Church Fathers. *An Exposition of the Orthodox Faith* Book I, (John Damascus). Available on http://www.newadvent.org/fathers/33041.htm Accessed on 18 June 2009.

Cawte, J. "Karl Rahner's Conception of God's Self Communication to Man." *Heythrop Journal* 25, no. 3 (1984): 260–271.

Danielou, J. *A History of the Christian Doctrine Before the Council of Nicea*, vol. I. Translated and edited by J. A. Baker. London: Darton, Longman and Todd, 1964.

———. *The Theology of Jewish Christianity.* Translated and edited by J. A. Baker. London: Darton, Longman and Todd, 1964.

Diop, C. A. *Precolonial Black Africa.* Brooklyn, New York: Lawrence Hill Books, 1987.

Dorrien, Gary J. *The Barthian Revolt in Modern Theology: Theology without Weapons.* Westminster: John Knox Press, 1999.

Dunn, J. D. G. *The Partings of the Ways.* London: SCM Press; Philadelphia: Trinity Press International, 1991.

Eichrodt, W. *Theology of the Old Testament.* Philadelphia: The Westminster Press, 1967.

Evans, C. A. *Ancient Texts for New Testament Studies: A Guide to the Background Literature.* Peabody, MA: Hendrickson Publishers, 2005.

———. "Was Simon ben Kosiba Recognized as Messiah?" In *Jesus and His Contemporaries: Comparative Studies*, edited by C. A. Evans, 183–211. Leiden: Brill, 1995.

Feldman, L. H. "Palestinian and Diaspora Judaism in the First Century." In *Christianity and Rabbinic Judaism: A Parallel History of Their Origins and Early Development*, edited by Hershel Shanks. Washington DC: Biblical Archeology Society, 1992.

Ferguson, E. *Backgrounds of Early Christianity.* Grand Rapids, MI: Eerdmans, 1987.

Fichte, J. G. *Science of Knowledge.* New York: Meredith, 1970.

Fortes, M., and E. E. Evans-Pritchard. *African Political Systems.* London: Oxford University Press, 1940.

Fuller, C. E. "God in African Thought and Life." In *God in Contemporary Thought: A Philosophical Perspective*, edited by S. Matczak, 19–47. New York: Learned Publications, 1977.

Green, M. *Evangelism in the Early Church.* Grand Rapids, MI: Eerdmans, 1971.

Green, W. S. "Messiah in Judaism: Rethinking the Question." In *Judaisms and their Messiahs at the Turn of the Christian Era*, edited by J. Neusner,

W. S. Green, and E. S. Freichs, 1–13. Cambridge: Cambridge University Press, 1987.

Gregory, Bishop of Nyssa. "Against Sabellius." In *Nicene and Post-Nicene Fathers of the Christian Church,* vol. IX, edited by P. Schaff. Grand Rapids, MI: Eerdmans, 1891.

Griaule, M. *Dieu d'eau: Entretiens avec Ogotommeli.* Paris: Editions du Chêne, 1948. English edition: *Conversations with Ogotommeli.* London: Oxford University Press, 1965.

Hall, C. "Adding Up Trinity." *Christianity Today* (28 April 1997): 26–28.

Hardy, D. W. "Created and Redeemed Society." In *On Being the Church: Essays on the Christian Community,* edited by Colin E. Gunton and Daniel W. Hardy. Edinburgh: T&T Clark, 1989.

Hegel, G. W. F. *Phenomenology of the Spirit.* Translated by A. V. Miller. Oxford: Clarendon Press, 1977.

Henle, R. J., *St Thomas and Platonism: A Study of the Plato and Platonici Texts in the Writings of St. Thomas.* The Hague: Martinus Nijhoff, 1956.

Henry, C. F. H. *God, Revelation and Authority Vol V: God Who Stands and Stays Part 1.* Waco, TX: World Book Publishing House, 1982.

Heureux, C. E. L. *Rank among the Canaanite Gods: El, Baal, and the Rephaim.* Ann Arbor, MI: Scholars Press, 1979.

Hilary, Bishop of Poitiers. "*De Trinitate.*" In *Nicene and Post-Nicene Fathers of the Christian Church,* vol. IX, edited by P. Schaff. Grand Rapids, MI: Eerdmans, 1891.

Hoernle, R. F. A. *Idealism as a Philosophical Doctrine.* London : Hodder and Stoughton Ltd, 1924.

Horbury, W. *Jewish Messianism and the Cult of the Christ.* London: SCM Press, 1998.

———. *Messianism among Jews and Christians: Twelve Biblical and Historical Studies.* London and New York: T. & T. Clark International, 2003.

Idowu, B. *Olódùmarè: God in Yoruba Belief.* London: Longmans, 1962.

Inwood, M. "Hegel." In *The Blackwell Companion to Philosophy,* edited by Nicholas Bunnin and E. P. Tsui-James. Oxford: Blackwell Publishers, 1996.

Isaac, B., and A. Oppenheimer, "The Revolt of Bar Kokhba: Ideology and Modern Scholarship." *Journal of Jewish Studies* 36, no. 1 (1985).

Jahn, J. *Muntu: An Outline of the New African Culture.* New York: Grove Press, 1961.

Johnson, E. A. "Naming God She: The Theological Implications." Boardman Lecture XXXVII (Centennial Lecture), Department of Religious Studies, University of Pennsylvania, presented on 19 October 2000.

Kain, P. J. "Self-Consciousness, the Other and Hegel's Dialectic of Recognition." *Philosophy and Social Criticism* 24, no. 5 (1998): 105–126.

Kalilombe, P. "Evangelization and the Holy Spirit." *African Ecclesial Review* 18 (1976): 8–18.

———. "The Salvific Value of the African Religions." *African Ecclesial Review* 21 (1979): 143–156.

Kant, I. *Critique of Pure Reason*. Translated by N. K. Smith. London: Palgrave Macmillan, 2007.

Kato, B. *Biblical Christianity in Africa*. Achimota, Ghana: Africa Christian Press, 1985.

———. *Theological Pitfalls*. Kisumu, Kenya: Evangel Publishing House, 1975.

Kerferd, G. B. "Aristotle." In *The Encyclopedia of Philosophy*, edited by P. Edwards. London: Macmillan, 1967.

Kibicho, S. "Revelation in African Religion." *Africa Theological Journal* 12 (1983): 3, 166–177.

———. "The Teaching of African Religion in Our Schools and Colleges and the Christian Attitude towards This Religion." *Africa Theological Journal* 10 (1981): 3, 29–37.

Kinoti, G. *Hope for Africa*. Nairobi: AISRED, 1994.

Kombo, J. H. O. *The Doctrine of God in African Christian Thought*. Leiden: Brill, 2007.

Laato, A. *A Star Is Rising: The Historical Development of the Old Testament Royal Ideology and the Rise of the Jewish Messianic Expectations*. USF International Studies in Formative Christianity and Judaism. Atlanta: Scholars Press, 1997.

Lang, A. *The Making of Religion*. London: Longmans, 1898.

Lasker D. J., *Jewish Philosophical Polemics Against Christianity in the Middle Ages*. New York: Ktav Pub House, 1977.

Latourette, K. S. *A History of Christianity: Volume I: Beginnings to 1500*. New York: HarperCollins, 1975.

———. *A History of the Expansion of Christianity*, Volume 1. Grand Rapids, MI: Zondervan Publishing House, 1970.

Lonergan, B. J. F. *The Way to Nicea. Dialectical Development of Trinitarian Theology*. Philadelphia: Westminster Press, 1976.

Lossky, V. *The Mystical Theology of the Eastern Church*. Crestwood, NY: St. Vladimir's Seminary Press, 1976.

Louth, A. *St. John Damascene: Tradition and Originality in Byzantine Theology*. Oxford, England: Oxford University Press, 2004.

Mackintosh, H. R. *The Christian Apprehension of God*, 4th ed. London: Student Christian Movement Press, 1934.

Magesa, L. "Evangelisation." *African Ecclesial Review* 24 (1982): 354–362.

———. "Who Are 'the People of God'?" *African Ecclesial Review* 26 (1984): 204–212.

Malcolm, Lois. "An Interview with David Tracy." *The Christian Century* (13–20 February 2002): 24–30. Accessed on 11 May 2009 on http://www.religion-online.org/showarticle.asp?title=2269.

Masolo, D. A. *African Philosophy in Search of Identity.* Bloomington, IN: Indiana University Press, 1994.

Mbiti, J. S. *African Religions and Philosophy.* London: Heinemann, 1969.

———. "The Holy Spirit in African Independent Churches." In *Festschrift Günther Wagner*, edited by Günter Wagner, 101–111. New York: Peter Lang, 1994.

———. *Introduction to African Religion.* London: Heinemann, 1975.

———. "Our Savior as an African Experience." In *Christ and Spirit in the New Testament*, edited by B. Lindars, S. Smalley, and C. F. D. Moule, 397–414. Cambridge: Cambridge University Press, 1973.

———. "Some Reflections on the African Experience of Salvation Today." In *Living Faiths and Ultimate Goals: A Continuing Dialogue*, edited by S. J. Samartha, 108–119. Geneva: WCC, 1974.

McFague, S. *Metaphorical Theology.* London: SCM Press, 1983.

McNamara, M. *Targum and Testament: Aramaic Paraphrases of the Hebrew Bible: A Light on the New Testament.* Grand Rapids, MI: Eerdmans, 1972.

McPherson, T. "Positivism and Religion." In *Religious Language and the Problem of Religious Knowledge,* edited by R. E. Santoni. Bloomington: Indiana University Press, 1968.

Miller, S. "The Utility and Importance of Creeds and Confessions." In *Doctrinal Integrity: On the Utility and Importance of Creeds and Confessions and Adherence to Our Doctrinal Standards*, edited S. Miller. Dallas: Presbyterian Heritage Publications, 1989.

Moltmann, J. *The Trinity and the Kingdom.* San Francisco: Harper and Row, 1981.

Mugambi, J. N. K. *The African Heritage and Contemporary Christianity.* Nairobi: Longman Kenya, 1989.

Mussner, Franz. *Tractate of the Jews: The Significance of Judaism for Christian Faith.* Philadelphia: Fortress Press; London: SPCK, 1984.

Nash, R. H. *The Light of the Mind: St Augustine's Theory of Knowledge.* Lexington, KY: The University Press of Kentucky, 1969.

Nasr, S. H. "Islamic Conception of Intellectual Life." In *Dictionary of History of Ideas II (638-652)*, edited by P. P. Wierner, 638–651. New York: Charles Scribner's Sons, 1973.

Nazianzen, St Gregory. "In sanct. bapt. *Oratio* XL, 43," P.G., XXXVI.

———. "Oratio XL, 41," P.G., XXXVI, 417 BC.

———. "Oratio XLV, 4," P.G., XXXV1, 628 C.

———. "Oratio XXXI (Theologica V), ix" P.G., XXXVI, 144 A.

———. "Orations". In *Nicene and post-Nicene Fathers of the Christian Church*, vol. IX, edited by P. Schaff. Grand Rapids, MI: Eerdmans, 1891.
Neusner, J. *Messiah in Context: Israel's History and Destiny in Formative Judaism*. Philadelphia: Fortress Press, 1984.
Neusner, J., W. S. Green, and E. S. Frerichs, eds. *Judaisms and Their Messiahs at the Turn of the Christian Era*. Cambridge: Cambridge University Press, 1987.
Newman, N. A., ed. *The Early Christian Muslim Dialogue: A Collection of Documents from the First Three Islamic Centuries (632-900)*. Hatfield, PA: Interdisciplinary Biblical Research Institute, 1993.
Nyamiti, C. *African Tradition and the Christian God*. Eldoret: Gaba Publications, 1979.
———. *The Way to Christian Theology for Africa*. Eldoret: Gaba Publications, 1978.
Okot p'Bitek. *African Religions in Western Scholarship*. Nairobi: Kenya Literature Bureau, 1970.
Omerald, N. "Wrestling with Rahner on the Trinity." *Irish Theological Quarterly* 68, no. 3 (2003): 213–227.
Origen. "On the Gospel of John." In *Ante-Nicene Fathers: Translations of the Writings of the Fathers Down to AD 325*, vol. III, edited by A. Roberts and J. Donaldson. Grand Rapids, MI: Eerdmans, 1951.
Pamphilus, E. *Ecclesiastical History*. Grand Rapids, MI: Baker Book House, 1966.
Pannenberg, W. *Systematic Theology*, 3 Vols. Translated by Geoffrey W. Bromiley. Grand Rapids, MI: Eerdmans, 1991–1998.
———. *Theology and the Kingdom of God*. Edited by Richard John Neuhaus. Philadelphia: Westminster Press, 1977.
Parrinder, E. G. *Africa's Three Religions*. London: Sheldon Press, 1969.
Pelikan, J. *The Christian Tradition*, vol I. Chicago: The University of Chicago Press, 1971.
Rahner, K. *Encyclopedia of Theology*. New York: Seabury, 1975.
———. *Foundations of Christian Faith: An Introduction to the Idea of Christianity*. Translated by W. V. Dych. New York: Seabury, 1978.
———. *Theological Investigations* I. Translated by C. Ernest. London: Darton, Longman and Todd, 1965.
———. *Theological Investigations* IV. Translated by K. Smyth. London: Darton, Longman and Todd, 1966.
———. *Theological Investigations* XI. London: Darton, Longman and Todd, 1974.
———. *The Trinity*. New York: Crossroad, 1970/1997.
Ramose, M. B. *African Philosophy through Maim*. Harare: Mond Books, 2002.
Reinhartz, A. "Rabbinic Perceptions of Simeon bar Kosiba." *Journal for the Study of Judaism* 20, no. 2 (1989): 171–194.

Ricoeur, Paul. *Being, Essence and Substance in Plato and Aristotle*, translated by David Pellauer and John Starkey. Cambridge: Polity, 2013.

Sanneh, L. *Whose Religion Is Christianity? The Gospel beyond the West.* Grand Rapids, MI: Eerdmans, 2003.

Scholem, G. "Toward Understanding the Messianic Idea in Judaism." In *The Messianic Idea in Judaism*, edited by G. Scholem, 1–36. New York: Schocken Books, 1971.

Scott, D. C. *Dictionary of the Nyanja Language.* Edited by A. Hetherwick. London: Religious Tract Society, 1929.

Setiloane, G. M. *African Theology: An Introduction.* Johannesburg: Skotaville Publishers, 1986.

———. *The Image of God among the Sotho-Tswana.* Rotterdam: Balkema, 1976.

———. "Modimo: God among the Sotho-Tswana." *Journal of Theology for Southern Africa* 4, no. 4 (September 1973): 6–17. Skarsaune, O. "Is Christianity Monotheistic? A Perspective on a Jewish/Christian Debate." *Studia Patristica* 29 (1957): 340–363.

Smith, E. W. *African Ideas of God.* London: Edinburgh House Press, 1950.

St Athanasius, "Contra Arianos, Oratio IV, i," P.G,, XXVI, 468 B.

St Basil of Caesarea. *De Spiritu Sancto.* Downloaded on 7 May 2009 at http://www.newadvent.org/fathers/3203.htm.

———. "St. Basil: Letters and Select Works." In vol. 8 of *A Select Library of Nicene and Post-Nicene Fathers of the Christian Church*, edited by Philip Schaff and Henry Wace. New York: The Christian Literature Company, 1890–1900.

Steyne, P. M. *Gods of Power: A Study of Beliefs and Practices of Animists.* Houston, TX: Touch Publications, 1989.

Tempels, P. *Bantu Philosophy.* Paris: Présence Africaine, 1969.

Tertullian. "*Adversus Iudaeus.*" (An Answer to the Jews, translated by S. Thelwal). In *Ante-Nicene Fathers: Translations of the Writings of the Fathers Down to AD 325,* vol. III, edited by A. Roberts and J. Donaldson. Grand Rapids, MI: Eerdmans, 1951.

———. "*Against Praxeas*" and "*De Carne Christi.*" Translated by D. Holmes. In *Ante-Nicene Fathers: Translations of the Writings of the Fathers Down to AD 325,* vol. III, edited by A. Roberts and J. Donaldson. Grand Rapids, MI: Eerdmans, 1951.

Teugels, L. "The Background of the Anti-Christian Polemics in Aggadat Bereshit." *Journal of the Study of Judaism* XXX, no. 2 (1999): 178–208.

Thackeray, H., trans. *Josephus III.* The Loeb Classical Library series, 210. London: Heinemann; Cambridge, MA: Harvard University Press, 1928.

Tillich, P. *Systematic Theology*, vol. I, II, III. Chicago: University of Chicago Press, 1951, 1957, 1963.

Torrance, T. F. *The Christian Doctrine of God, One Being Three Persons.* Edinburgh: T & T Clark, 1996.

———. *The Trinitarian Perspective: Toward Doctrinal Agreement.* Edinburgh: T&T Clark, 1994.

Tylor, E. B. *Primitive Culture: Researches into Development of Mythology, Philosophy, Religion, Language, Art, and Custom.* New York: Holt: 1889.

Valliere, Paul. *Modern Russian Theology: Bukharev, Soloviev, Bulgakov: Orthodox Theology in a New Key.* Edinburgh: T. & T. Clark, 2000.

van Binsbergen, W. M. J. "Reconciliation: A Major African Social Technology of Shared and Recognised Humanity (Ubuntu)." Paper presented at the "Seminar on Culture and Globalization," Human Sciences Research Council, Pretoria, 21 April 1999.

Van Rooy, J. A. *The Traditional World View of the Black People in Southern Africa.* Potchefstroom: Instituut vir die Bevordering van Calvinisme, 1978.

Wainwright A. W, *The Trinity in the New Testament.* London: SPCK, 1962.

Walls, A. F. "The Great Commission 1910-2010." Lecture delivered at the University of Edinburgh, 2002. http://www.towards2010.org.uk/downloads/t2010paper01walls.pdf. Accessed on 8 May 2009.

Wolfson, H. A. "The Muslim Attributes and the Christian Trinity." *The Harvard Theological Review* 49 (1956): 1–18.

———. *The Philosophy of Church Fathers: Faith, Trinity and Incarnation.* Cambridge, MA: Harvard University Press, 1970.

———. *The Philosophy of the Kalam.* Cambridge, MA: Harvard University Press, 1976.

World Missionary Conference 1910. Report of Commission I: *Carrying the Gospel to All the Non-Christian World.* Edinburgh: Oliphant, Anderson and Ferrier, 1910.

Wright, G. E. *The Biblical Doctrine of Man and Society.* London: SCM Ltd., 1954.

Yandell, K. E. "The Most Brutal and Inexcusable Error in Counting: Trinity and Consistency." *Religious Studies* 30, no. 2 (1994): 201–217.

Zizioulas, J. D. *Being as Communion: Studies in the Personhood of the Church.* Crestwood, NY: St Vladimir's Seminary Press, 1985.

———. "The Doctrine of the Holy Trinity: The Significance of the Cappadocian Contribution." In *Trinitarian Theology Today*, edited by C. Schwöbel. Edinburgh: T. & T. Clark, 1995).

———. "The Teaching of the 2$^{nd}$ Council on the Holy Spirit in Historical and Ecumenical Perspective." In *Credo in Spiritum Sanctum*, vol. 1, edited by J. S. Martins, 29–54. Rome: Libreria Editrice Vaticana, 1983.

# Index

Abelard, Peter  58, 63
Adeyemo, Tokunboh  9
Agbasiere, Joseph Thérèse  9
Anderson, J. F.  59
Anselm  58, 63
Apostel  101, 103
Aquinas, Thomas  5, 16, 49, 54, 55, 56, 58, 59, 60, 61, 62, 63
Aristotle  42, 49, 54, 55, 56, 58, 59, 95
Arius  40, 45, 46, 89
Athanasius  39, 84, 92, 107
Augustine  5, 13, 16, 39, 49, 50, 51, 52, 54, 61, 62, 74
Bacon  65
Barth, Christoph  104
Barth, Karl  11, 12, 16, 70, 71, 80
Battaglia, Vincent  78
Bediako, K.  41
Behrend, H.  113
Benedict of Aniane  63
Berkhof, H.  60, 62
Blommendaal, J.  104
Boehme, Jacob  85
Boethius  5, 16, 49, 54, 56, 63
Boff, Leonardo  93, 94
Bonhoeffer, Dietrich  80
Bosch, D. J.  104
Bourke, V. F.  59
Bruce, F. F.  14
Brunner  80

Bulgakov, Sergius  84, 85, 91, 92, 93
Bultmann  80
Bunnin, Nicholas  66
Butler, D. J.  66, 68, 69
Byabazaire, Deogratias M.  9
Byaruhanga-Akiiki, Anatole  9
Callaway, H.  116
Calvin, J.  5, 112
Cappadocian Fathers  4
Cappadocians  39, 112
Cawte, John  77
Charlesworth, J. H.  24
Clement  13
Coffey, David  81
Cross, F. M.  104
Cusa, Nicholas of  69
Damascus, John  107
Deren, Maya  100
Descartes  65, 66, 68, 69
Dieterlen  100
Diop, C. A.  100, 101
Donaldson, J.  35
Dunn, J. D. G.  26
Edwards, P.  54
Eichrodt, W.  28, 29, 31, 32, 120
Eissfeldt, Otto  104
Evans, C. A.  22, 26
Evans-Pritchard, E. E.  100
Feldman, Louis H.  21, 22
Ferguson, Everett  21, 23
Fichte, J. G.  65, 66

Fortes, M. 100
Freedman, H. 34
Frerichs, E. P. 24
Gabriel Satilaone 97
Gavin D'Costa 81
Gemser, B. 104
Georg Fohrer 104
Green, M. 13, 14
Green, W. S. 24, 26
Griaule, M. 100
Gunton, Colin E. 4
G. W. Bromiley 104
Hall, C. 2
Hardy, Daniel W. 3, 4
Hegel, G. W. F. 65, 66, 68, 69
Henle, R. J. 58
Henry, C. F. H. 1, 2
Heureux, C. E. L. 104
Hilary, Bishop of Poitiers 110
Hoernle, R. F. A. 65
Holmes, D. 35
Horbury, W. 24
Hugh of St Victor 58
Idowu, B. 97
Inwood, M. 66, 68, 69
Isaac, B. 26
Jacobi, Friedrich Heinrich 65
Jahn, J. 100, 101, 104
Jenkins, Philip 99
Johnson, Elizabeth 2, 3
Justin Martyr 26, 33
Kagame, Alexis 100, 101, 103
Kain, P. J. 68
Kalilombe, Patrick 9
Kant, Immanuel 65, 66, 67
Kato, Byang 9
Kerferd, G. B. 54
Kibicho, Samuel 9
Kinoti, G. 98, 99
Kombo, J. H. O. 35, 97
Laato, A. 23

Lang, Andrew 10
Lasker, D. J. 58
Latourette, Kenneth Scott 13, 14, 41
Lindars, B. 9
Lonergan, B. J. F. 39
Lossky, V. 42, 43, 44, 83, 84, 85, 86, 87, 88, 89, 90, 92
Louth, Andrew 43, 44
Lucian of Antioch 40
Lucretius 95
Mackintosh, H. R. 42
Magesa, Laurenti 9
Magnus, Albertus 63
Malcolm, Lois 95
Masolo, D. A. 100, 101, 103
Matczak, S. 11
Mbiti, J. S. 9, 97, 100, 101, 103, 110, 111, 112, 115
McFague, S. 5
McNamara, M. 30
McPherson, Thomas 3
Miller, A. V. 68
Miller, S. 5, 45, 46, 47, 48
Moltmann, J. 71, 80, 93, 94
Moule, C. F. D. 9
Mugambi, J. N. K. 113
Mulder, M. J. 104
Mussner, Franz 26
Nash, R. H. 51
Nasr, S. H. 57
Nazianzen, Gregory 42, 84, 87, 88, 89, 90, 92, 93, 107
Neusner, J. 24, 26
Newman, N. A. 57
Niebuhr, R. 80
Nietzsche, F. 95
Noetus 41
Nyamiti, Charles 9
Nyssa, Gregory of 107
Okot p'Bitek 9
O'Meara, J. J. 59

Omerald, N. 78
Oppenheimer, A. 26
Origen 13, 35
Pamphilus, Eusebius 13
Pannenberg, W. 93, 94
Parrinder, E. G. 103, 104
Pegis, A. C. 59
Pelikan, J. 1
Philo 22, 29, 34, 50
Plato 49, 50, 55, 58, 85
Plotinus 49, 51, 53, 83
Pope Calixtus 41
Rabbi Johanan 34
Rahner, K. 16, 61, 70, 74, 75, 76, 77, 78, 80, 81, 105, 106
Ramose, M. B. 100
Rand, E. K. 54
Reinhartz, A. 26
Reinhold, Karl Leonhard 65
Rendtorff, Rolf 104
Ricoeur, Paul 49
Roberts, A. 35
Robertson, Ian W. 11
Sabellius 40, 107
Samartha, S. J. 9
Samosata, Paul of 40
Sanneh, Lamin 101, 105
Santoni, R. E. 3
Satiloane, M. 105
Schaff, P. 42, 51, 107, 110
Schelling, Friedrich 65
Schleiermacher, Friedrich 65
Scholem, G. 26
Schulze, Gottlob Ernst 65
Schwöbel, C. 108
Scott, D. C. 104, 105
Scotus Erigna, John 63
Setiloane, G. M. 105
Simon, M. 34
Skarsaune, O. 33, 34, 35, 56, 57
Smalley, S. 9

Smith, E. W. 104
St Basil 4, 5, 92, 111, 112
Stewart, H. F. 54
Steyne, P. 104
St John Damascene 88, 89, 90
Tempels, P. 100, 101, 102, 104, 112, 118, 119
Tertullian 13, 14, 35, 39, 41
Teugels, L. 35
Thackeray, H. 25
Thelwal, S. 35
Thielicke 80
Tillich 80
Torrance, T. F. 6, 18, 19, 80, 107
Tracy, David 95
Trypho 33, 34
Tsui-James, E. P. 66
Tylor, E. B. 97
Valliere, Paul 91
van Binsbergen, W. 100
van Rooy, J. A. 117
Wace, Henry 111
Wainwright, A. W. 31
Walls, Andrew F. 98
Waterhouse, Eric 10
Wierner, P. P. 57
William of Conches 58
Wolfson, H. A. 35, 56, 57
Wright, G. Ernest 12
Yandell, K. E. 2
Zabajungu, Boniface K. 9
Zizioulas, John D. 84, 89, 108

Langham Literature and its imprints are a ministry of Langham Partnership.

Langham Partnership is a global fellowship working in pursuit of the vision God entrusted to its founder John Stott –

> *to facilitate the growth of the church in maturity and Christ-likeness through raising the standards of biblical preaching and teaching.*

**Our vision** is to see churches in the majority world equipped for mission and growing to maturity in Christ through the ministry of pastors and leaders who believe, teach and live by the Word of God.

**Our mission** is to strengthen the ministry of the Word of God through:
- nurturing national movements for biblical preaching
- fostering the creation and distribution of evangelical literature
- enhancing evangelical theological education

especially in countries where churches are under-resourced.

**Our ministry**

*Langham Preaching* partners with national leaders to nurture indigenous biblical preaching movements for pastors and lay preachers all around the world. With the support of a team of trainers from many countries, a multi-level programme of seminars provides practical training, and is followed by a programme for training local facilitators. Local preachers' groups and national and regional networks ensure continuity and ongoing development, seeking to build vigorous movements committed to Bible exposition.

*Langham Literature* provides majority world preachers, scholars and seminary libraries with evangelical books and electronic resources through publishing and distribution, grants and discounts. The programme also fosters the creation of indigenous evangelical books in many languages, through writer's grants, strengthening local evangelical publishing houses, and investment in major regional literature projects, such as one volume Bible commentaries like *The Africa Bible Commentary* and *The South Asia Bible Commentary*.

*Langham Scholars* provides financial support for evangelical doctoral students from the majority world so that, when they return home, they may train pastors and other Christian leaders with sound, biblical and theological teaching. This programme equips those who equip others. Langham Scholars also works in partnership with majority world seminaries in strengthening evangelical theological education. A growing number of Langham Scholars study in high quality doctoral programmes in the majority world itself. As well as teaching the next generation of pastors, graduated Langham Scholars exercise significant influence through their writing and leadership.

To learn more about Langham Partnership and the work we do visit **langham.org**

www.ingramcontent.com/pod-product-compliance
Lightning Source LLC
Chambersburg PA
CBHW051944160426
43198CB00013B/2285